编写委员会

总 主 编：郁云峰

副总主编：于天琪　陈维昌

主　　编：马　祯　李英芹

副 主 编：邢二军　贾勇骁

编　　者：安启启　王　宝　包　娟　郭红娟　李剑雄　张俊文

编辑委员会

主　　　任：陈维昌

副 主 任：付彦白

项目负责人：付彦白

项 目 秘 书：武传霞

项 目 审 定：王俊毅

项 目 成 员：武传霞　王巧燕　方兴龙　赫　栗　张　彪

专家委员会（按音序排列）

陈曼倩　哈尔滨职业技术大学　　　　崔永华　北京语言大学

梁赤民　中国－赞比亚职业技术学院　梁　宇　北京语言大学

刘建国　哈尔滨职业技术大学　　　　宋继华　北京师范大学

宋　凯　有色金属工业人才中心　　　苏英霞　北京语言大学

赵丽霞　有色金属工业人才中心

职通中文

Access to Vocational Chinese

煤矿开采技术

Coal Mining Technology

郁云峰　总主编

于天琪　陈维昌　副总主编

兰州资源环境职业技术大学　编

初级篇

Elementary

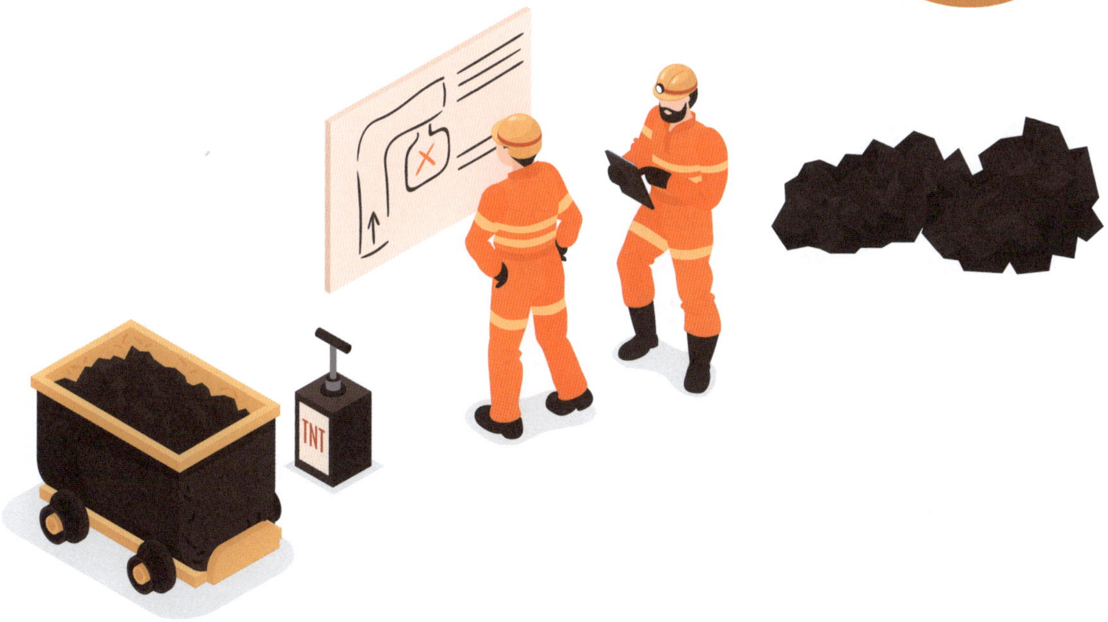

北京语言大学出版社

BEIJING LANGUAGE AND CULTURE UNIVERSITY PRESS

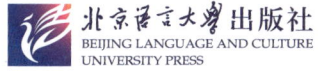

©2025北京语言大学出版社，社图号24183

图书在版编目（CIP）数据

煤矿开采技术. 初级篇 / 郁云峰总主编；兰州资源环境职业技术大学编. -- 北京：北京语言大学出版社，2025.5. --（"职通中文"系列教材）. -- ISBN 978-7-5619-6662-4

Ⅰ. H195.4

中国国家版本馆CIP数据核字第20242CW134号

煤矿开采技术（初级篇）
MEIKUANG KAICAI JISHU（CHUJIPIAN）

责任编辑：	王巧燕　张　彪
英文编辑：	侯晓娟　翟世权
排版制作：	北京创艺涵文化发展有限公司
责任印制：	周　燚

出版发行：	北京语言大学出版社
社　　址：	北京市海淀区学院路15号，100083
网　　址：	www.blcup.com
电子信箱：	service@blcup.com
电　　话：	编辑部　8610-82303647/3592/3395
	国内发行　8610-82303650/3591/3648
	海外发行　8610-82303365/3080/3668
	北语书店　8610-82303653
	网购咨询　8610-82303908
印　　刷：	北京瑞禾彩色印刷有限公司

版　　次：2025年5月第1版		**印　　次**：2025年5月第1次印刷	
开　　本：787毫米×1092毫米 1/16		**印　　张**：20.5	
字　　数：234千字			
定　　价：115.00元			

PRINTED IN CHINA

凡有印装质量问题，本社负责调换。售后QQ号1367565611，电话 010-82303590

前 言

为进一步推动各国学习者中文语言能力和专业技能深度融合，提升学习者围绕特定行业场景、典型工作任务使用中文进行沟通和交流的能力，持续满足中文学习者的职业规划和个人发展需求，实现优质教育资源共享，促进多彩文明交流互鉴，教育部中外语言交流合作中心联合有色金属工业人才中心，根据各国"中文＋职业技能"教学发展实际需求，以中国职业院校为依托，组织职业教育、国际中文教育、出版和相关企业等领域的专家，共同研发"职通中文"系列教材及配套教学资源。

"职通中文"系列教材参照《国际中文教育中文水平等级标准》和《职业中文能力等级标准》，分为初、中、高三个等级。各等级均遵循"语言和技能相融合""好学、好教、好用"的编写理念，根据相关职业的典型工作场景、工作任务和高频用语，设计课文、会话、语言点和练习等板块，不断提升学习者在职业技术领域的中文应用水平和关键技术能力，为学习者尽快熟悉和适应工作环境提供帮助。本系列教材适用于在中国企业从事相关职业工作的各国员工，也适用于在华留学生或长短期培训人员，以及有意向了解中国语言文化和职业技能的学习者。

《煤矿开采技术（初级篇）》是"职通中文"系列丛书之一，可用于中国"走出去"企业从事煤矿开采岗位的本土员工在岗语言和技术培训。通过学习本教材，学习者能够提升中文交际能力、技能操作水平，在从事煤矿开采相关工作中能够与中国员工或客户用中文进行简单的工作交流，掌握简单的煤矿开采技术专业词汇，以及煤矿开采全流程操作技巧。

本教材共分34课，包括煤矿生产安全基础知识、矿井通风、煤矿开采、煤炭运输、巷道掘进等井下生产作业过程的要求及相关设备的操作方法。本教材旨在在工作流程中融入煤矿开采的实际场景，使学习者能够根据自己的工作岗位有针对性地开展学习。本教材在编写过程中，充分运用了企业调研、资源收集、专家咨询等方式，项目团队为每个工作任务确定了12～15个高频词汇，结合煤矿开采过程中常用的短语、短句，配以语法、现场图片和日常习惯用语等内容，力图以图文并茂的形式呈现真实的职业场景，帮助学习者掌握在职业场景中用中文进行基本交际的能力。

学习者学习本教材后应当可以：

1. 掌握煤矿开采过程中常用的基本词汇；
2. 能够和中国员工进行简单的工作交流；
3. 了解煤矿生产过程中的安全注意事项；
4. 了解煤矿生产设备在使用过程中的操作步骤；
5. 懂得与中国员工沟通交流时存在的文化差异。

本教材由兰州资源环境职业技术大学马祯院长、李英芹担任主编，邢二军、贾勇骁担任副主编，安启启、王宝、包娟、郭红娟、李健雄、张俊文等参与编写。具体分工为：马祯负责教材大纲编写及课文审核工作，李英芹负责教材编写及组织协调工作，邢二军、贾勇骁负责教材编写及统稿工作，安启启、王宝、包娟、郭红娟、张俊文负责各章节的编写工作，李健雄负责语法编写工作。

本教材得到了宋凯、赵丽霞、张琳、陆怀平等领导的关心和支持，崔永华、苏英霞、梁宇、宋继华、刘建国、梁赤民、陈曼倩等专家学者提出了许多宝贵建议，我们在此表示衷心感谢。本教材还得益于兰州资源环境职业技术大学和北京语言大学出版社的大力支持和精心指导，在此一并表示感谢。

"职通中文"系列教材的出版和应用能够促进各国"中文＋职业技能"人才的培养，推动当地经济发展，从而为构建人类命运共同体做出积极贡献。由于项目团队学识和相关经验有限，加之时间紧迫，本教材肯定有许多疏漏、不足之处。恳请本教材的使用者将发现的问题反馈给我们，以便再版和编写相关教材时改进。

编写团队

2023年11月

Preface

In order to further promote the deep integration of Chinese language proficiency and professional skills among learners from various countries and enhance their ability to communicate and interact in Chinese in specific industry scenarios and typical work tasks, the Center for Language Education and Cooperation under the Ministry of Education, in collaboration with China Nonferrous Metal Industry Talent Center, has organized experts from vocational education, international Chinese education, publishing, and related enterprises to jointly develop the "Access to Vocational Chinese" series of textbooks and supporting teaching resources. Based on the actual needs of "Chinese + Vocational Skills" teaching development in various countries and relying on Chinese vocational colleges, the series aims to continuously meet the career planning and personal development needs of Chinese learners, realize the sharing of high-quality educational resources, and promote exchanges and mutual learning among diverse civilizations.

In reference to *Chinese Proficiency Grading Standards for International Chinese Language Education* and *Chinese Proficiency Standards for Vocational Education*, the "Access to Vocational Chinese" series of textbooks is divided into three levels: elementary, intermediate, and advanced. All the levels follow the writing philosophy of "integrating language and skills" and "being easy to learn, teach, and use." The textbooks are designed around typical work scenarios, work tasks, and high-frequency terms of relevant professions, with sections on texts, conversations, language points, and exercises, continuously improving learners' Chinese application skills and key technical abilities in the vocational and technical fields, providing assistance for learners to quickly familiarize themselves with and adapt to the work environment. This series of textbooks is suitable for international employees engaged in relevant professions in Chinese companies, international students or trainees in China, as well as learners interested in Chinese language, culture, and vocational skills.

Coal Mining Technology (Elementary) is one of the "Access to Vocational Chinese" series, which can be used for on-the-job language and technical training of local employees engaged in coal mining in Chinese "going global" enterprises. After learning this textbook, learners can improve their Chinese communication skills and technical operation proficiency. They will be able to communicate in Chinese with Chinese employees or customers in work related to coal mining, master the simple specialized vocabulary of coal mining, and the whole process operation skills in coal mining.

The textbook is divided into 34 lessons, including the basic safety knowledge of coal mining production, the requirements of underground production operation process such as mine ventilation, coal mining, coal transportation, tunnel excavation, and the operation methods of related equipment. This textbook aims to integrate the actual scene of coal mining into the workflow, so that learners can carry out targeted learning according to their own jobs. In the process of compiling this textbook, methods such as enterprise investigation, resource collection and expert consultation were used. The project team determined 12-15 high-frequency words for each work task, combined with commonly used phrases, short sentences, and supplemented by grammar, on-site pictures and daily idioms in the process of coal mining. It endeavors to present authentic professional environments through integrated textual and visual media, helping learners to develop fundamental Chinese communicative competence in vocational settings.

After learning this textbook, learners should be able to:

1. Master the basic vocabulary commonly used in coal mining process;

2. Engage in simple work communication with Chinese employees;

3. Understand the safety precautions in the process of coal mining production;

4. Understand the operation steps of coal mining production equipment during use;

5. Understand the cultural differences when communicating with Chinese employees.

The editors-in-chief of this textbook are Dean Ma Zhen and Li Yingqin of Lanzhou Resource and Environment Vocational and Technical University, with Xing Erjun and Jia Yongxiao serving as deputy editors, and An Qiqi, Wang Bao, Bao Juan, Guo Hongjuan, Li Jianxiong, Zhang Junwen, and others participating in the writing. They respectively did the following jobs: Ma Zhen is responsible for writing outline of the textbook and reviewing the text, Li Yingqin is responsible for the compilation and coordinating of the textbook, Xing Erjun and Jia Yongxiao are responsible for the compilation and unification of the textbook, An Qiqi, Wang Bao, Bao Juan, Guo Hongjuan, and Zhang Junwen are responsible for writing each chapter, and Li Jianxiong is responsible for writing grammar.

We'd like to express our heartfelt thanks to Song Kai, Zhao Lixia, Zhang Lin,

Preface

Lu Huaiping, and other leaders for their concern and support of this textbook, and Cui Yonghua, Su Yingxia, Liang Yu, Song Jihua, Liu Jianguo, Liang Chimin, Chen Manqian and other experts and scholars for their valuable suggestions. Thanks also go to Lanzhou Resource and Environment Vocational and Technical University and Beijing Language and Culture University Press for their support and guidance.

The publication and application of the "Access to Vocational Chinese" series of textbooks aim to develop talents with "Chinese + Vocational Skills" across the globe, promote local economies, and make positive contributions to building a community with a shared future. Due to limited knowledge and related experience of the project team, as well as time constraints, this textbook is bound to have many deficiencies that need improvement. We sincerely invite users of this textbook to provide feedback on any issues discovered, so that we can make improvements in future editions and related materials.

Compiling Team
November 2023

词类简称表
List of Abbreviations of Parts of Speech

词性 Part of speech	英译 English	简称 Abbreviation
名词 míngcí	noun	*n.*
专有名词 zhuānyǒu míngcí	proper noun	*pn.*
代词 dàicí	pronoun	*pron.*
数词 shùcí	numeral	*num.*
量词 liàngcí	measure word	*m.*
数量词 shùliàngcí	quantifier	*q.*
动词 dòngcí	verb	*v.*
能愿动词 néngyuàn dòngcí	optative	*opt.*
形容词 xíngróngcí	adjective	*adj.*
副词 fùcí	adverb	*adv.*
介词 jiècí	preposition	*prep.*
连词 liáncí	conjunction	*conj.*
助词 zhùcí	particle	*part.*
叹词 tàncí	interjection	*int.*
前缀 qiánzhuì	prefix	*pref.*
后缀 hòuzhuì	suffix	*suf.*
短语 duǎnyǔ	phrase	*phr.*

目 录 Contents

第 1 课　认识煤炭　　　　　　　Lesson 1　Learn the Coal ············ 1

第 2 课　认识煤矿　　　　　　　Lesson 2　Learn the Coal Mine ······ 9

第 3 课　安全培训　　　　　　　Lesson 3　Safety Training ··········· 17

第 4 课　准备下井　　　　　　　Lesson 4　Preparation Before Going down the Shaft ·········· 26

第 5 课　认识巷道　　　　　　　Lesson 5　Learn the Tunnel ········ 34

第 6 课　使用自救器　　　　　　Lesson 6　The Use of the Self-Rescuer ················· 44

第 7 课　检查矿灯　　　　　　　Lesson 7　Check the Miner's Lamp ···················· 53

第 8 课　乘坐罐笼　　　　　　　Lesson 8　Ride the Cage ············ 62

第 9 课　乘坐猴车　　　　　　　Lesson 9　Ride the Monkey Car ··· 72

第 10 课　井下行走　　　　　　　lesson 10　Walk During Downhole Work ················· 82

第 11 课　通过风门　　　　　　　lesson 11　Pass Through the Damper ···················· 91

第 12 课　检查瓦检仪光路　　　　Lesson 12　Check the Light Path of the Gas Detector ······ 101

第 13 课　检查瓦检仪气密性　　　Lesson 13　Check the Airtightness of the Gas Detector ······ 111

第 14 课　检查瓦检仪药品　　　　Lesson 14　Check the Medication of the Gas Detector ······ 121

第 15 课　检查瓦斯气体浓度　　　Lesson 15　Check the Gas Concentration ········ 131

第 16 课 测风前的准备	Lesson 16 Preparation Before Wind Measurement ········ 140
第 17 课 测风的方法	lesson 17 Anemometry Method ····················· 149
第 18 课 检查煤电钻	Lesson 18 Check the Electric Coal Drill ················ 158
第 19 课 操作煤电钻	Lesson 19 Operate the Electric Coal Drill ················ 167
第 20 课 关停煤电钻	Lesson 20 Shut down the Electric Coal Drill ············· 176
第 21 课 装雷管	Lesson 21 Install the Blasting Cap ····················· 185
第 22 课 装炸药	Lesson 22 Load Explosives ······· 194
第 23 课 连线	Lesson 23 Connection ············ 204
第 24 课 起爆	Lesson 24 Detonation ············ 212
第 25 课 启动局部通风机	Lesson 25 Start the Local Ventilating Fan ················ 221
第 26 课 安装锚杆	Lesson 26 Install the Anchor Rod ····················· 230
第 27 课 检查皮带运输机	Lesson 27 Check the Belt Conveyor ····················· 239
第 28 课 检查掘进机	Lesson 28 Check the Tunneling Machine ············· 249
第 29 课 启动掘进机	Lesson 29 Start the Tunneling Machine ············· 259
第 30 课 关停掘进机	Lesson 30 Shut down the Tunneling Machine ············· 268
第 31 课 检查采煤机	Lesson 31 Check the Coal Mining Machine ············· 277

目 录 Contents

第 32 课　启动采煤机　　　　　　Lesson 32　Start the Coal Mining Machine ················ 286

第 33 课　关停采煤机　　　　　　Lesson 33　Shut down the Coal Mining Machine ······ 295

第 34 课　启动刮板运输机　　　　Lesson 34　Start the Scraper Conveyor ················ 303

第 1 课 Lesson 1

Rènshi méitàn
认识煤炭
Learn the Coal

 **热身 Warm-up**

下列图片你认识多少？ How many of the following pictures do you know?

méitàn
煤炭
coal

hēisè
黑色
black

zhíwù
植物
plant

ránshāo
燃烧
burn

kuàngwù
矿物
mineral

fādiàn
发电
power generation

学习生词 Words and Expressions 🎧 01-01

1	认识	rènshi	v.	learn
2	煤炭	méitàn	n.	coal
3	是	shì	v.	is, am, are
4	黑色	hēisè	n.	black
5	的	de	part.	used after an attribute to modify a noun
6	矿物	kuàngwù	n.	mineral
7	植物	zhíwù	n.	plant
8	变化	biànhuà	v.	change
9	形成	xíngchéng	v.	form
10	可以	kěyǐ	opt.	can
11	燃烧	ránshāo	v.	burn
12	和	hé	conj.	and
13	发电	fā//diàn	v.	generate power
14	重要	zhòngyào	adj.	important
15	资源	zīyuán	n.	resource

第 1 课 | 认识煤炭

词语练习 Word Exercises

1. 看图片，将相应的字母填在括号里。Look at the pictures and fill in the corresponding letters in the brackets.

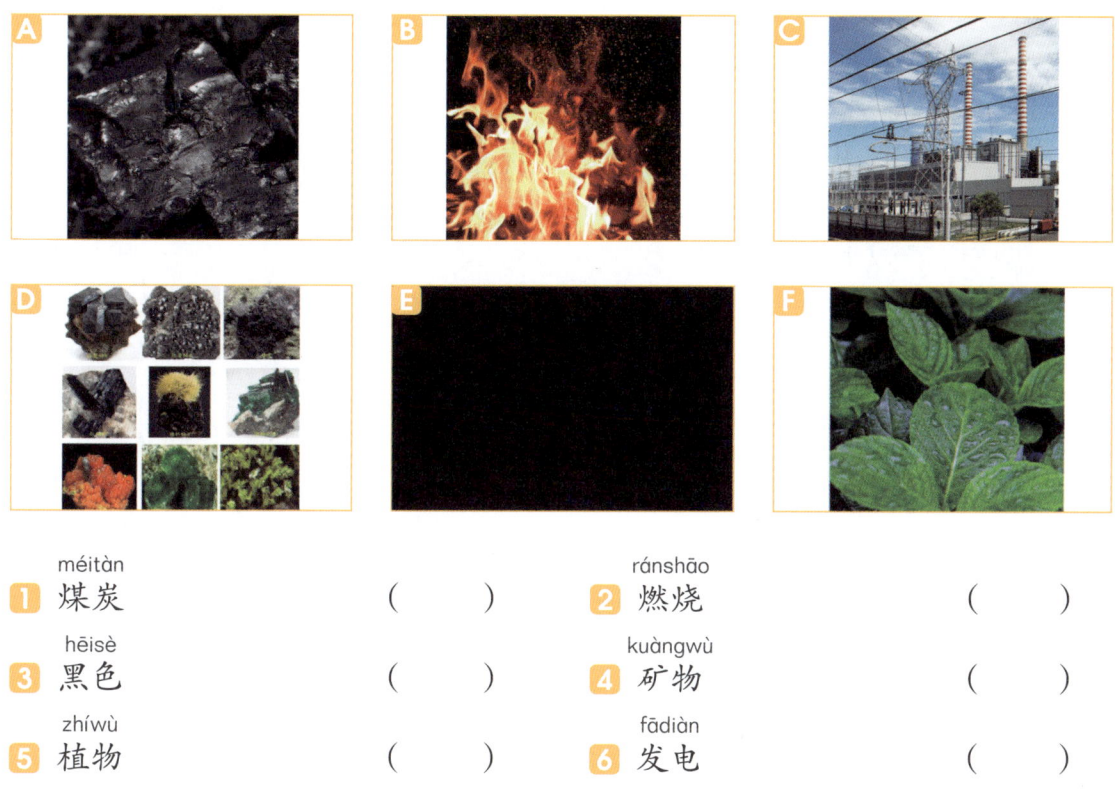

① méitàn 煤炭 ( )	② ránshāo 燃烧 ( )
③ hēisè 黑色 ( )	④ kuàngwù 矿物 ( )
⑤ zhíwù 植物 ( )	⑥ fādiàn 发电 ( )

2. 朗读词语搭配。Read aloud the word collocations.

① 认识	认识煤炭	② 可以	可以燃烧
	认识植物		可以发电
③ 形成	形成煤炭	④ 燃烧	植物燃烧
	形成矿物		矿物燃烧

3

学习课文 Text 🎧 01-02

认识煤炭
Rènshi méitàn

Méitàn shì hēisè de kuàngwù. Zhíwù biànhuà xíngchéng méitàn.
煤炭是黑色的矿物。植物变化形成煤炭。

Méitàn kěyǐ ránshāo hé fādiàn, shì zhòngyào de zīyuán.
煤炭可以燃烧和发电，是重要的资源。

Learn the Coal

The coal is a black mineral. It is formed by plant changes. The coal can be burned and used for power generation, and it is an important resource.

课文练习 Text Exercises

1. 根据课文内容，判断对错。Tell True (T) or False (F) according to the text.

Statements	Answer	
❶ 煤炭是黑色的矿物。	A. 是	B. 不是
❷ 煤炭可以燃烧。	A. 是	B. 不是
❸ 煤炭可以发电。	A. 是	B. 不是
❹ 植物变化形成煤炭。	A. 是	B. 不是

第1课 | 认识煤炭

2. 根据课文内容，选词填空。Choose the words to fill in the blanks according to the text.

1️⃣ _____是黑色的_____。　　A. 矿物　　B. 煤炭

2️⃣ _____变化形成煤炭。　　　　A. 植物　　B. 矿物

3️⃣ 煤炭可以燃烧和_____。　　　A. 发电　　B. 形成

4️⃣ 煤炭是重要的_____。　　　　A. 变化　　B. 资源

学习语法 Grammar

语法点 1 Grammar Point 1

"是"字句　"是" - Sentences

用于表达对某物属性、特征等的判断。结构为"A 是 B"，否定形式为"A 不是 B"。

It is used to indicate a judgment on the attributes, features, etc. of something. Its structure is "A 是 B". Its negative form is "A 不是 B".

Méitàn shì kuàngwù.
1️⃣ 煤炭是 矿物。The coal is a mineral.

Méitàn shì hēisè de kuàngwù.
2️⃣ 煤炭是黑色的 矿物。The coal is a black mineral.

Méitàn shì zhòngyào de zīyuán.
3️⃣ 煤炭是 重要 的 资源。The coal is an important resource.

5

语法点1练习 Grammar Point Exercises 1

连词成句。Rearrange the words to form sentences.

1. ①重要的　②煤炭　③是　④资源

2. ①煤炭　②矿物　③是

3. ①矿物　②是　③煤炭　④黑色的

4. ①植物　②煤炭　③是　④不

语法点2 Grammar Point 2

能愿动词：可以　The optative verb: 可以

表示可能或能够。
It indicates the possibility or ability.

1. Méitàn kěyǐ ránshāo.
   煤炭可以燃烧。The coal can be burned.

2. Méitàn kěyǐ fādiàn.
   煤炭可以发电。The coal can be used for power generation.

3. Zhíwù kěyǐ xíngchéng méitàn.
   植物可以形成煤炭。Plants can form the coal.

语法点2练习 Grammar Point Exercises 2

连词成句。Rearrange the words to form sentences.

1. ①发电　②可以　③煤炭

2. ①燃烧　②可以　③煤炭

3. ①煤炭　②形成　③可以　④植物

4. ①资源　②是　③煤炭　④重要的

第1课 | 认识煤炭

汉字书写 Writing Chinese Characters

文化拓展 Culture Insight

Overview about China

The People's Republic of China, abbreviated as "China", is one of the oldest countries across the world. It is a multi-ethnic country with the Han ethnic group as the main ethnic group, and the Chinese language and Chinese characters are widely used. China is currently the most populous developing country (UN World Population Prospects, 2022) and the second largest economy in the world, ranking third globally in terms of the land area. China is a socialist country of the people's democratic dictatorship, and the socialism with Chinese characteristics has entered a new era after long-term efforts.

小结 Summary

词语 Words

连线。Match.

煤炭	mineral
植物	black
黑色	power generation
燃烧	burn
发电	plant
矿物	coal

语法 Grammar

朗读下面的句子。Read aloud the following sentences.

1. 煤炭是黑色的矿物。
2. 煤炭是重要的资源。
3. 煤炭可以燃烧和发电。
4. 植物变化形成煤炭。

课文理解 Text Comprehension

复述课文内容。Retell the text.

煤炭是黑色的_____。_____变化形成煤炭。煤炭可以_____和_____，是重要的_____。

第 2 课 Lesson 2
认识煤矿
Rènshi méikuàng
Learn the Coal Mine

 复习 Revision

连线。Match.

植物		burn
煤炭		power generation
发电		mineral
矿物		coal
燃烧		plant

9

 **热身 Warm-up**

下列图片你认识多少？How many of the following pictures do you know?

hàngdào
巷道
tunnel

méikuàng
煤矿
coal mine

shèbèi
设备
equipment

gōngzuòmiàn
工作面
working face

kāicǎi
开采
mining

 **学习生词 Words and Expressions** 🎧 02-01

1	煤矿	méikuàng	n.	coal mine
2	开采	kāicǎi	v.	mine
3	场所	chǎngsuǒ	n.	place
4	一般	yìbān	adj.	general
5	分为	fēnwéi	phr.	be divided into
6	井工	jǐnggōng	adj.	underground mining
7	露天	lùtiān	adj.	open-cut
8	中国	Zhōngguó	n.	China

第 2 课 | 认识煤矿

9	大部分	dàbùfen	n.	a majority of
10	由	yóu	prep.	by
11	巷道	hàngdào	n.	tunnel
12	设备	shèbèi	n.	equipment
13	工作面	gōngzuòmiàn	n.	working face
14	组成	zǔchéng	v.	consist of

词语练习 Word Exercises

1. 朗读词语搭配。Read aloud the word collocations.

❶ 煤矿	井工煤矿	❷ 开采	开采煤炭
	露天煤矿		开采煤矿
❸ 设备	使用（shǐyòng, use）设备	❹ 场所	工作（gōngzuò, work）场所
	检修（jiǎnxiū, overhaul）设备		开采场所

2. 连线。Match.

巷道　　　　　　　　　　　　　　　　equipment

煤矿　　　　　　　　　　　　　　　　working face

设备　　　　　　　　　　　　　　　　coal mine

工作面　　　　　　　　　　　　　　　tunnel

学习课文 Text 🎧 02-02

认识煤矿
Rènshi méikuàng

煤矿是开采煤炭的场所，一般分为井工煤矿和露天煤矿。中国大部分煤矿是井工煤矿。煤矿由巷道、设备和工作面组成。

Learn the Coal Mine

Coal mines are places for mining the coal, and they can be generally divided into underground coal mines and open-cut coal mines. A majority of coal mines in China are underground coal mines. Coal mines consist of tunnels, equipment, and working faces.

课文练习 Text Exercises

1. 根据课文内容，判断对错。Tell True (T) or False (F) according to the text.

Statements	Answer	
① 煤矿分为井工煤矿和露天煤矿。	A. 是	B. 不是
② 煤矿是开采煤炭的场所。	A. 是	B. 不是
③ 煤矿由巷道和设备组成。	A. 是	B. 不是
④ 中国大部分煤矿是露天煤矿。	A. 是	B. 不是

2. 根据课文内容，选词填空。Choose the words to fill in the blanks according to the text.

① _____是开采_____的场所。　　A. 煤矿　　B. 煤炭

② 煤矿分为_____和_____。　　　A. 露天煤矿　B. 井工煤矿

③ 煤矿由巷道、_____和工作面_____。A. 组成　　B. 设备

④ 中国_____煤矿是井工煤矿。　　　A. 大部分　B. 开采

学习语法 Grammar

语法点 1 Grammar Point 1

结构助词：的　The structural particle: 的

用于连接定语与中心语。常用结构为"定语 + 的 + 中心语"。

It is used to connect an attributive with its headword. The common structure is "attributive + 的 + headword".

Méikuàng shì kāicǎi méitàn de chǎngsuǒ.
① 煤矿 是 开采 煤炭 的 场所。Coal mines are places for mining the coal.

Jiàoshì shì shàngkè de chǎngsuǒ.
② 教室 是 上课 的 场所。Classrooms are places for having classes.

Tā shì wǒmen de Zhōngwén lǎoshī.
③ 他是我们的 中文 老师。He is our Chinese language teacher.

语法点 1 练习 Grammar Point Exercises 1

连词成句。Rearrange the words to form sentences.

① ①上课　②是　③的　④教室　⑤场所

② ①我们　②汉字　③学习　④的　⑤声调

③ ①他们　②同学　③我　④是　⑤的

④ ①发音　②你　③的　④注意（zhùyì, pay attention to）

语法点 2 Grammar Point 2

固定格式：由……组成　The fixed pattern: 由……组成
用于表示几个部分构成一个整体。
It is used to indicate that several parts form a whole thing.

① Méikuàng yóu hàngdào、shèbèi hé gōngzuòmiàn zǔchéng.
煤矿 由 巷道、设备 和 工作面 组成。Coal mines consist of tunnels, equipment, and working faces.

② Kuàng zì yóu shí hé guǎng zǔchéng.
"矿"字由"石"和"广"组成。The character "矿" consists of "石" and "广".

③ Hǎo zì yóu nǚ hé zǐ zǔchéng.
"好"字由"女"和"子"组成。The character "好" consists of "女" and "子".

语法点 2 练习 Grammar Point Exercises 2

用"由……组成"改写句子。Rewrite the sentences with "由……组成".

① 巷道、设备和工作面组成煤矿。

② "女"和"子"组成"好"字。

③ "石"和"广"组成"矿"字。

④ 姓和名组成姓名。

第 2 课 | 认识煤矿

汉字书写 Writing Chinese Characters

职业拓展 Career Insight

Coal Classification

  The coal can be divided into four categories: peat, lignite, bituminous coal, and anthracite coal according to the degree of coalification. Humans had recording of using coal as early as the Neolithic. Coal mining in China must be performed in accordance with the law, and the procedures must be complete and valid. We must implement the safety production policy of "safety first, prevention oriented, and comprehensive management".

小结 Summary

词语 Words

根据课文内容，选择恰当的词语。Choose the appropriate words according to the text.

煤矿是开采煤炭的_____，一般分为井工煤矿和露天煤矿。中国_____煤矿是_____煤矿。煤矿由巷道、设备和_____组成。

A. 场所　　　B. 工作面　　　C. 井工　　　D. 大部分

语法 Grammar

用"组成""的"填空。Fill in the blanks with "组成" and "的".

1 煤矿是开采煤炭_____场所。　　　A. 组成　　B. 的

2 教室是上课_____场所。　　　　　A. 组成　　B. 的

3 煤矿由巷道、设备和工作面_____。　A. 组成　　B. 的

4 "矿"字由"石"和"广"_____。　　　A. 组成　　B. 的

课文理解 Text Comprehension

复述课文内容。Retell the text.

煤矿是开采煤炭的_____，一般分为_____和_____。煤矿由_____、_____和_____组成。

第 3 课 / Lesson 3
Ānquán péixùn
安全培训
Safety Training

复习 Revision

连线。Match.

煤矿　　　　巷道　　　　工作面　　　　设备　　　　开采

热身 Warm-up

下列图片你认识多少？ How many of the following pictures do you know?

hégézhèng
合格证
certificate

ānquán péixùn
安全 培训
safety training

gōngrén
工人
worker

17

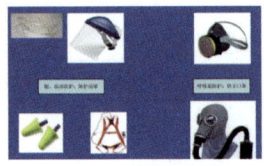
fánghù yòngpǐn
防护 用品
protective equipment

kǎoshì
考试
examination

ānquán zhīshi
安全 知识
safety knowledge

 学习生词 Words and Expressions 🎧 03-01

1	安全培训	ānquán péixùn	*phr.*	safety training
2	工人	gōngrén	*n.*	worker
3	必须	bìxū	*adv.*	must
4	参加	cānjiā	*v.*	participate in
5	通过	tōngguò	*v.*	pass
6	考试	kǎoshì	*n.*	examination
7	取得	qǔdé	*v.*	obtain
8	合格证	hégézhèng	*n.*	certificate
9	后	hòu	*n.*	then
10	才	cái	*adv.*	*used to indicate that something happens only on certain conditions*
11	下井	xià jǐng	*phr.*	go down the shaft
12	内容	nèiróng	*n.*	content
13	包括	bāokuò	*v.*	include
14	安全知识	ānquán zhīshi	*phr.*	safety knowledge
15	防护用品	fánghù yòngpǐn	*phr.*	protective equipment

第 3 课 | 安全培训

16	使用	shǐyòng	v.	use
17	井下	jǐngxià	phr.	under the shaft
18	应急措施	yìngjí cuòshī	phr.	emergency measure

词语练习 Word Exercises

1. 朗读词语搭配。Read aloud the word collocations.

❶	参加	参加培训	❷	井下	井下防护用品
		参加考试			井下应急措施
❸	安全	安全知识	❹	通过	通过考试
		安全培训			通过培训

2. 连线。Match.

安全培训　　　　　　　　　　　　　　　　　certificate

合格证　　　　　　　　　　　　　　　　　　protective equipment

工人　　　　　　　　　　　　　　　　　　　worker

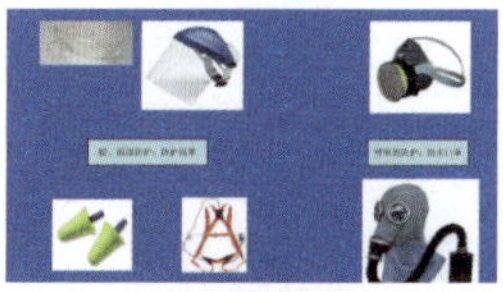

防护用品　　　　　　　　　　　　　　　　　safety training

学习课文 Text 🎧 03-02

安全培训 Ānquán péixùn

煤矿工人必须参加安全培训，通过考试，取得合格证后才可以下井。培训内容包括煤矿安全知识、煤矿防护用品的使用和井下应急措施。

Safety Training

Coal mine workers must participate in safety training and pass the examination, and then obtain the certificate before their downhole work. The training content includes coal mine safety knowledge, the use of coal mine protective equipment, and downhole emergency measures.

课文练习 Text Exercises

1. 根据课文内容，判断对错。Tell True (T) or False (F) according to the text.

Statements	Answer
❶ 煤矿工人必须参加安全培训。	A. 是　　B. 不是

② 煤矿工人必须参加考试。	A. 是	B. 不是
③ 煤矿工人取得合格证后才可以下井。	A. 是	B. 不是
④ 煤矿培训内容包括安全知识。	A. 是	B. 不是

2. 根据课文内容，选词填空。Choose the words to fill in the blanks according to the text.

① 煤矿 _____ 必须参加 _____。　　A. 安全培训　B. 工人

② 煤矿工人 _____ 通过 _____。　　A. 必须　　　B. 考试

③ 培训内容包括煤矿 _____ 和井下 _____。A. 应急措施　B. 安全知识

④ 煤矿工人取得 _____ 后才可以 _____。A. 下井　　　B. 合格证

学习语法 Grammar

 语法点1 Grammar Point 1

副词：必须　The adverb: 必须

用在动词前，表示事理上和情理上必要。

It is used before a verb to indicate both objective and emotional necessities.

- Gōngrén bìxū cānjiā ānquán péixùn.
① 工人必须参加安全培训。Workers must participate in safety training.

- Gōngrén bìxū cānjiā ānquán kǎoshì.
② 工人必须参加安全考试。Workers must take a safety exam.

- Gōngrén bìxū qǔdé hégézhèng.
③ 工人必须取得合格证。Workers must obtain a certificate of qualification.

第3课 | 安全培训

21

语法点1练习 Grammar Point Exercises 1

连词成句。Rearrange the words to form sentences.

1. ①参加　②工人　③安全培训　④必须

_____

2. ①参加　②必须　③工人　④安全考试

_____

3. ①取得　②合格证　③工人　④必须

_____

4. ①安全知识　②学习　③工人　④必须

_____

语法点2 Grammar Point 2

副词：才　The adverb: 才

表示必要的、唯一的条件。
It indicates necessary and unique conditions.

1. Méikuàng gōngrén qǔdé hégézhèng hòu cái kěyǐ xià jǐng.
   煤矿 工人 取得 合格证 后才可以下井。Coal miners can only enter the mine after obtaining a certificate of qualification.

2. Gōngrén tōngguò kǎoshì cái kěyǐ qǔdé hégézhèng.
   工人 通过 考试才可以取得合格证。Workers need to pass an exam to obtain a certificate of qualification.

3. Xuéshēng tōngguò kǎoshì cái kěyǐ bìyè.
   学生 通过 考试才可以毕业。Students need to pass exams to graduate.

语法点 2 练习 Grammar Point Exercises 2

用"才"改写句子。Rewrite the sentences with "才".

1. 煤矿工人通过安全考试可以下井。

2. 学生通过考试可以毕业。

3. 工人取得合格证可以参加工作。

4. 工人参加培训可以了解安全知识。

汉字书写 Writing Chinese Characters

职业拓展 Career Insight

The Coal Mining History in Ancient China

China is one of the countries with the richest coal resources in the world, with coal being a key resource in China's energy structure. China boasts thousands of years of coal mining history and is one of the earliest countries in the world to discover and utilize the resource, which is a fact known by few people. As early as around 500 BC during the Spring and Autumn Period and the Warring States Period, coal had become an important product, known as black stone. It was known as charcoal during the Tang Dynasty, and then referred to as coal during the Ming Dynasty. Today, coal remains a vital part of our daily lives, and coal mining holds great importance in the national economy.

小结 Summary

词语 Words

根据课文内容，选择恰当的词语。Choose the appropriate words according to the text.

煤矿工人必须参加_____，通过考试，取得合格证后才可以_____。培训内容包括煤矿安全知识、煤矿_____的使用和井下_____。

A. 防护用品　　B. 下井　　C. 安全培训　　D. 应急措施

语法 Grammar

用"必须""才"填空。Fill in the blanks with "必须" or "才".

1. 工人_____参加安全培训。　　A. 必须　　B. 才
2. 工人_____参加安全考试。　　A. 必须　　B. 才
3. 煤矿工人取得合格证_____可以下井。　　A. 必须　　B. 才
4. 工人通过考试_____可以取得合格证。　　A. 必须　　B. 才

课文理解 Text Comprehension

复述课文内容。Retell the text.

  煤矿工人必须参加_____，通过考试，取得_____后才可以下井。培训内容包括煤矿_____、煤矿_____的使用和井下_____。

第 4 课 Lesson 4

Zhǔnbèi xià jǐng
准备下井
Preparation Before Going down the Shaft

复习 Revision

连线。Match.

安全培训　工人　合格证　安全知识　防护用品　考试

 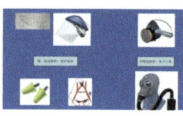 

热身 Warm-up

下列图片你认识多少？ How many of the following pictures do you know?

ānquánmào
安全帽
safety helmet

gōngzuòfú
工作服
work clothes

kuàngdēng
矿灯
miner's lamp

第4课 | 准备下井

jiāoxuē
胶靴
rubber boots

pídài
皮带
belt

zìjiùqì
自救器
self-rescuer

 学习生词 Words and Expressions 🎧 04-01

1	准备	zhǔnbèi	v.	prepare
2	前	qián	n.	before
3	工作	gōngzuò	n.	work
4	穿	chuān	v.	put on
5	工作服	gōngzuòfú	n.	work clothes
6	胶靴	jiāoxuē	n.	rubber boots
7	戴	dài	v.	wear
8	安全帽	ānquánmào	n.	safety helmet
9	脖子	bózi	n.	neck
10	上	shang	n.	on, above
11	系	jì	v.	tie
12	条	tiáo	m.	*a measure word for towels*
13	毛巾	máojīn	n.	towel
14	腰	yāo	n.	waist

27

15	皮带	pídài	n.	belt
16	个	gè	m.	*a measure word*
17	矿灯	kuàngdēng	n.	miner's lamp
18	自救器	zìjiùqì	n.	self-rescuer

词语练习 Word Exercises

1. 朗读词语搭配。Read aloud the word collocations.

❶ 穿	穿工作服	❷ 戴	戴安全帽
	穿胶靴		
❸ 系	系毛巾	❹ 一条	一条毛巾
	系皮带		一条皮带

2. 连线。Match.

工作服   safety helmet

胶靴   rubber boots

安全帽   work clothes

矿灯   miner's lamp

第4课 准备下井

学习课文 Text 🎧 04-02

准备下井
Zhǔnbèi xià jǐng

Xià jǐng qián de zhǔnbèi gōngzuò:
下井前的准备工作：

1. Bìxū chuān gōngzuòfú hé jiāoxuē, dài ānquánmào.
   必须穿工作服和胶靴，戴安全帽。

2. Bózi shang jì yì tiáo máojīn, yāo shang jì yì tiáo pídài.
   脖子上系一条毛巾，腰上系一条皮带。

3. Pídài shang jì yí gè kuàngdēng hé yí gè zìjiùqì.
   皮带上系一个矿灯和一个自救器。

Preparation Before Going down the Shaft

Preparation before downhole work:

1. The workers must put on his/her work clothes and rubber boots, and wear a safety helmet.

2. The worker ties a towel on the neck and fastens a belt on the waist.

3. The worker ties a miner's lamp and a self-rescuer on the belt.

课文练习 Text Exercises

1. 根据课文内容，判断对错。Tell True (T) or False (F) according to the text.

Statements	Answer
❶ 煤矿工人下井前必须穿工作服吗？	A. 是　　B. 不是

② 煤矿工人下井前必须穿胶靴、戴安全帽吗？	A. 是	B. 不是
③ 煤矿工人下井前脖子上必须系一条毛巾吗？	A. 是	B. 不是
④ 煤矿工人下井前必须带矿灯和自救器吗？	A. 是	B. 不是

2. 根据课文内容，选词填空。Choose the words to fill in the blanks according to the text.

① _____下井前必须穿_____。　　A. 工作服　　B. 煤矿工人

② 煤矿工人下井前必须穿工作服和_____，戴_____。

　　A. 安全帽　　　　　B. 胶靴

③ 煤矿工人_____上系一条_____。　　A. 脖子　　B. 毛巾

④ 煤矿工人_____系一条_____。　　A. 腰上　　B. 皮带

学习语法 Grammar

语法点 1　Grammar Point 1

方位名词：上　The word of locality: 上

表示在身体、物体上方或者表面。

It indicates being above or on the surface of the body or object.

---

① Bózi shang jì yì tiáo máojīn.
　脖子 上 系一条毛巾。Tie a towel on the neck.

② Yāoshang jì yì tiáo pídài.
　腰 上 系一条皮带。Fasten a belt on the waist.

③ Pídài shang jì yí gè kuàngdēng.
　皮带 上 系一个 矿灯。Tie a miner's lamp on the belt.

语法点1练习 Grammar Point Exercises 1

连线，组成句子。 Match to form sentences.

脖子上　　　　　　　　　　　　系一个矿灯

腰上　　　　　　　　　　　　　系一条皮带

皮带上　　　　　　　　　　　　系一个自救器

　　　　　　　　　　　　　　　系一条毛巾

语法点2 Grammar Point 2

量词：条 The measure word: 条

用于计量条状的东西。
It is used to measure something strip-shaped.

1. Bózi shang jì yì tiáo máojīn.
   脖子上系一条毛巾。Tie a towel around the neck.
2. Yāo shang jì yì tiáo pídài.
   腰上系一条皮带。Tie a belt around the waist.
3. Xià jǐng gōngrén dài yì tiáo máojīn.
   下井工人带一条毛巾。The employee who goes down the shaft brings a towel.

语法点1练习 Grammar Point Exercises 1

用"条"改写下列句子。 Rewrite the following sentences with "条".

1. 脖子上系毛巾。_____
2. 腰上系皮带。_____
3. 下井工人带毛巾。_____
4. 煤矿下有巷道。_____

 ## 汉字书写 Writing Chinese Characters

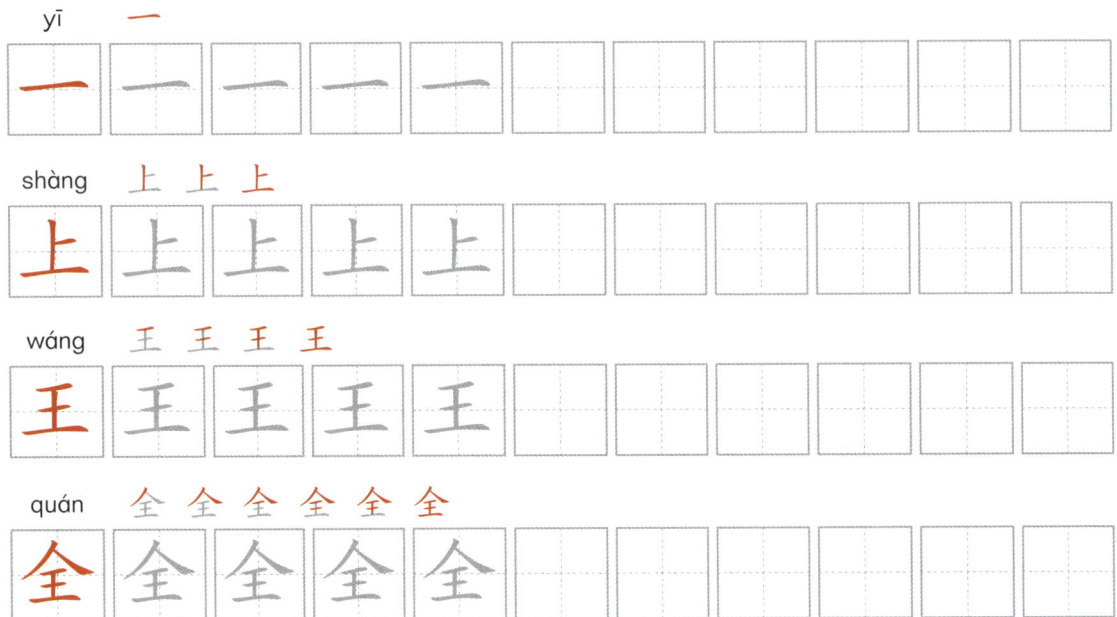

 ## 职业拓展 Career Insight

Notice for Downhole Work

Do not bring cigarettes, matches and lighters into the place of downhole work. Before the downhole work, check your pocket and place the igniter in a safe place on the well to avoid fire and gas explosions. Before the downhole work, do not drink alcohol, which may cause mental confusion and accidents.

小结 Summary

词语 Words

根据课文内容，选择恰当的词语。Choose the appropriate words according to the text.

下井前必须穿工作服和胶靴，戴_____。脖子上系一条_____，腰上系一条皮带。矿灯和_____系在_____上。

A. 安全帽　　　B. 自救器　　　C. 皮带　　　D. 毛巾

语法 Grammar

用"条""上"填空。Fill in the blanks with "条" or "上".

1. 下井前，脖子_____系一条毛巾。　　A. 上　　B. 条
2. 煤矿工人下井前，头_____戴安全帽。　　A. 上　　B. 条
3. 腰上系一_____皮带。　　A. 上　　B. 条
4. 工人皮带_____必须系矿灯。　　A. 上　　B. 条

课文理解 Text Comprehension

复述课文内容。Retell the text.

煤矿工人下井前，必须穿_____和_____，戴_____。脖子上系一条_____，_____系一条皮带。皮带上系一个_____和一个_____。

第 5 课 Lesson 5

认识巷道 Rènshi hàngdào
Learn the Tunnel

 复习 Revision

连线。Match.

矿物　　　　　　rubber boots

胶靴　　　　　　belt

安全帽　　　　　miner's lamp

皮带　　　　　　work clothes

工作服　　　　　safety helmet

第 5 课 | 认识巷道

热身 Warm-up

下列图片你认识多少？ How many of the following pictures do you know?

hàngdào
巷道
tunnel

gǒngxíng
拱形
arch

dòngshì
硐室
chamber

dìxià
地下
underground

páishuǐ
排水
drainage

学习生词 Words and Expressions 🎧 05-01

1	为了	wèile	*prep.*	for
2	从	cóng	*prep.*	from
3	地面	dìmiàn	*n.*	ground
4	向	xiàng	*prep.*	to
5	地下	dìxià	*n.*	underground
6	开掘	kāijué	*v.*	excavate

35

7	各类	gè lèi	*phr.*	all sorts of
8	通道	tōngdào	*n.*	passageway
9	硐室	dòngshì	*n.*	chamber
10	叫	jiào	*v.*	be called
11	用来	yònglái	*phr.*	be used for
12	运输	yùnshū	*v.*	transport
13	通风	tōng//fēng	*v.*	ventilate
14	行人	xíng rén	*phr.*	people's passing-through
15	排水	pái//shuǐ	*v.*	drain
16	按	àn	*prep.*	according to
17	形状	xíngzhuàng	*n.*	shape
18	梯形	tīxíng	*n.*	trapezoid
19	矩形	jǔxíng	*n.*	rectangle
20	拱形	gǒngxíng	*n.*	arch
21	圆形	yuánxíng	*n.*	circle

词语练习 Word Exercises

1. 看图片，将相应的字母填在括号里。 Look at the pictures and fill in the corresponding letters in the brackets.

A

B

C

第 5 课 | 认识巷道

1. 地下（　　）　　2. 巷道（　　）　　3. 拱形（　　）
4. 通风（　　）　　5. 排水（　　）　　6. 通道（　　）
7. 地面（　　）　　8. 硐室（　　）　　9. 梯形（　　）
10. 开掘（　　）　　11. 运输（　　）　　12. 圆形（　　）

2. 朗读词语搭配。Read aloud the word collocations.

巷道	梯形巷道	trapezoidal tunnel
	拱形巷道	arched tunnel
	矩形巷道	rectangular tunnel
	圆形巷道	circular tunnel
	水平巷道	horizontal tunnel
	倾斜巷道	inclined tunnel
	开拓巷道	development tunnel
	回采巷道	mining tunnel

37

学习课文 Text 🎧 05-02

认识巷道
Rènshi hàngdào

为了开采煤炭，从地面向地下开掘的各类通道和硐室叫巷道，用来运输煤炭、通风、行人和排水。巷道按形状可以分为梯形巷道、矩形巷道、拱形巷道和圆形巷道。

Learn the Tunnel

In order to perform coal mining, all sorts of passageways and chambers excavated from the ground to the underground are called tunnels, which are used for coal transportation, ventilation, people's passing-through, and drainage. Tunnels can be divided by shape into trapezoidal tunnels, rectangular tunnels, arched tunnels, and circular tunnels.

课文练习 Text Exercises

1. 根据课文内容，判断对错。**Tell True (T) or False (F) according to the text.**

Statements	Answer
❶ 开掘巷道是为了开采煤炭。	A. 是　　B. 不是

第 5 课 | 认识巷道

② 拱形和梯形是巷道的形状。	A. 是	B. 不是
③ 巷道是从地下向地面开掘的通道。	A. 是	B. 不是
④ 巷道可以排水、通风、行人、运输煤炭。	A. 是	B. 不是

2. 根据课文内容，选词填空。Choose the words to fill in the blanks according to the text.

① 巷道的形状有拱形、矩形、（   ）、圆形。
A. 正方形　　　　B. 梯形　　　　　C. 五边形

② 行人、运输煤炭、排水的通道叫（   ）。
A. 巷道　　　　　B. 马路　　　　　C. 桥

③ 巷道是从地面向地下开掘的（   ）。
A. 通道　　　　　B. 矿物　　　　　C. 梯形

④ 为了（   ）煤炭，煤矿工人开掘了巷道。
A. 开掘　　　　　B. 开采　　　　　C. 通风

 学习语法 Grammar

 语法点 1 Grammar Point 1

介词：为了　The preposition: 为了

表示目的与行为的关系。常用结构为"为了 + 目的 + 行为"。
It indicates the relationship between the purpose and the behavior. The common structure is "为了 + purpose + behavior".

　　　　Wèile kāicǎi méitàn,　rénmen kāijuéle hàngdào.
① 为了开采煤炭，人们开掘了巷道。People excavate tunnels to perform coal mining.

39

>   Wèile tōngguò kǎoshì, tóngxuémen nǔlì xuéxí.
> ❷ 为了通过考试，同学们努力学习。Students study hard to pass the examinations.
>
>   Wèile ānquán, méikuàng gōngrén xià jǐng qián bìxū qǔdé hégézhèng.
> ❸ 为了安全，煤矿工人下井前必须取得合格证。For safety reasons, coal miners must obtain a certificate of qualification before going down the shaft.

语法点1练习 Grammar Point Exercises 1

连线，组成句子。Match to form sentences.

为了安全　　　　　　　　同学们必须通过考试

为了毕业　　　　　　　　煤矿工人必须通过考试

为了发电　　　　　　　　他看中文电影（diànyǐng, movie）

为了练习中文　　　　　　人们开采煤矿

语法点2 Grammar Point 2

> **固定格式：从……向……**　　The fixed pattern: 从……向……
>
> 用于表示动作的起点和方向。常用结构为"从 + 名词 + 向 + 名词 + 动词性成分"。
>
> It is used to indicate the starting point and direction of an action. The common structure is "从 + noun + 向 + noun + verbal element".
>
> ---
>
>   Cóng dìmiàn xiàng dìxià kāijué tōngdào.
> ❶ 从地面向地下开掘通道。Excavate tunnels from the ground to the underground.
>
>   Cóng dìxià xiàng dìmiàn yùnshū méitàn.
> ❷ 从地下向地面运输煤炭。Transport coal from the underground to the ground.
>
>   Wǒmen cóng xià xiàng shàng kàn.
> ❸ 我们从下向上看。We look from bottom to top.

第 5 课 | 认识巷道

语法点 2 练习 Grammar Point Exercises 2

连词成句。Rearrange the words to form sentences.

1. ①地下　②从　③地面　④排水　⑤向

2. ①地面　②从　③向　④煤炭　⑤地下　⑥运输

3. ①向　②地面　③从　④开掘　⑤地下　⑥巷道

4. ①你　②后　③向　④看　⑤前　⑥从

汉字书写 Writing Chinese Characters

sì

zhōng

zhī

hàng

41

 ## 文化拓展 Culture Insight

Ying Zheng, the First Emperor of Qin

Ying Zheng (259 BC–210 BC), the first emperor of Qin, was an outstanding statesman, strategist and reformer in ancient China. He put Li Si, Wang Jian, etc. in important positions and conquered six states of Han, Zhao, Wei, Chu, Yan, and Qi successively from 230 BC to 221 BC, completing the great cause of unifying China and establishing a centralized and unified multi-ethnic state—Qin. As he was the first monarch in Chinese history to use the title of emperor, he was called Qinshihuang.

 ## 小结 Summary

词语 Words

根据课文内容，选择恰当的词语。Choose the appropriate words according to the text.

为了开采煤炭，从 _____ 向地下 _____ 的各类 _____ 和硐室叫巷道，用来运输煤炭、_____、行人和排水。

A. 开掘　　　B. 通风　　　C. 通道　　　D. 地面

语法 Grammar

朗读下面的句子。Read aloud the following sentences.

 为了开采煤炭，人们开掘巷道。

2 为了安全，煤矿工人必须取得合格证。

3 从地面向地下开掘通道。

4 我们从上向下看。

课文理解 Text Comprehension

根据课文内容，判断对错。Tell True (T) or False (F) according to the text.

从地面向地下开掘的通道是巷道。 A passage dug from the ground to the underground is a tunnel.	A. 是　　B. 不是
硐室是排水、通风、运输煤炭的通道。 The chamber is a channel for drainage, ventilation and transportation of coal.	A. 是　　B. 不是
巷道可以用来运输煤炭。 The tunnel can be used to transport coal.	A. 是　　B. 不是
巷道不可以是圆形的通道。The tunnel cannot be a circular channel.	A. 是　　B. 不是

第 6 课 使用自救器
Lesson 6 — Shǐyòng zìjiùqì
The Use of the Self-Rescuer

 复习 Revision

连线。 Match.

中文	图	English
硐室		underground
排水		arch
地下		drainage
巷道		tunnel
拱形		chamber

44

 **热身 Warm-up**

下列图片你认识多少？ How many of the following pictures do you know?

qìpíng
气瓶
air bottle

kāiguān
开关
switch

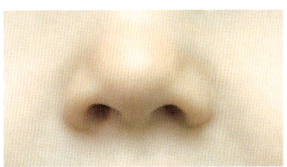
bíkǒng
鼻孔
nostril

zuǐ
嘴
mouth

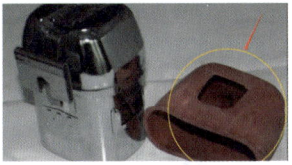
bǎohùzhào
保护罩
protective cover

hūxī
呼吸
breathe

 **学习生词 Words and Expressions**  06-01

1	步骤	bùzhòu	n.	step
2	取下	qǔxia	phr.	remove
3	保护罩	bǎohùzhào	n.	protective cover
4	打开	dǎ//kāi	v.	open
5	气瓶	qìpíng	n.	air bottle
6	开关	kāiguān	n.	switch
7	拿住	názhù	phr.	hold

8	口具	kǒujù	n.	mouthpiece
9	放入	fàngrù	phr.	put
10	中	zhōng	n.	in
11	咬住	yǎozhù	phr.	grip...with teeth
12	用	yòng	prep.	use
13	鼻夹	bíjiā	n.	nose clip
14	夹住	jiāzhù	phr.	clamp
15	鼻孔	bíkǒng	n.	nostril
16	开始	kāishǐ	v.	start
17	好	hǎo	adj.	good
18	嘴	zuǐ	n.	mouth
19	呼吸	hūxī	v.	breathe

词语练习 Word Exercises

1. 连线。Match.

气瓶   nostril

开关   mouth

鼻孔   air bottle

嘴   switch

2. 朗读词语搭配。Read aloud the word collocations.

❶ 取	取安全帽	❷ 夹住	夹住皮带
	取保护罩		夹住鼻孔
❸ 打开	打开气瓶	❹ 用……呼吸	用鼻呼吸
	打开开关		用嘴呼吸

 学习课文 Text 06-02

使用自救器
Shǐyòng zìjiùqì

使用自救器的步骤：

1. 取下保护罩，打开气瓶开关。
2. 拿住口具，放入口中，咬住口具。
3. 用鼻夹夹住鼻孔，开始用嘴呼吸。
4. 戴好安全帽。

The Use of the Self-Rescuer

Steps for using the self-rescuer:

1. Remove the protective cover and turn on the switch of the air bottle.
2. Hold the mouthpiece, put it in the mouth and grip it tightly with teeth.

3. Use the nose clip to clamp the nostrils and begin to use your mouth to breathe.

4. Wear the safety helmet properly.

课文练习 Text Exercises

1. 根据课文内容，判断对错。 Tell True (T) or False (F) according to the text.

Statements	Answer	
❶ 使用自救器要（yào, need）取下保护罩。	A. 是	B. 不是
❷ 使用自救器要打开气瓶开关。	A. 是	B. 不是
❸ 使用自救器要用鼻夹夹住鼻孔。	A. 是	B. 不是
❹ 使用自救器要用嘴呼吸。	A. 是	B. 不是

2. 根据课文内容，选词填空。 Choose the words to fill in the blanks according to the text.

❶ 取下 _____，打开 _____ 开关。　　A. 气瓶　　B. 保护罩

❷ 拿住 _____，放入口中，_____ 口具。　A. 口具　　B. 咬住

❸ 用鼻夹夹住 _____，开始用嘴 _____。　A. 呼吸　　B. 鼻孔

❹ 戴好 _____。　　　　　　　　　　　　A. 安全帽　B. 煤矿职工

学习语法 Grammar

语法点 1 Grammar Point 1

动词 + 下 / 住 / 好　Verb + 下 / 住 / 好

"下""住""好"用在动词后，表示动作的结果。

"下"，"住"，or "好" is used after a verb to indicate the result of an action.

　　　　Qǔxia　zìjiùqì　de bǎohùzhào.
① 取下自救器的保护罩。Remove the protective cover of the self-rescuer.

　　　　Shǐyòng　zìjiùqì　bìxū yǎozhù kǒujù.
② 使用 自救器必须咬住口具。Grip the mouthpiece tightly with teeth when using the self-rescuer.

　　　　Xià jǐng　bìxū dàihǎo ānquánmào.
③ 下 井 必须戴好 安全帽。Do wear the safety helmet properly for the downhole work.

语法点1练习 Grammar Point Exercises 1

选词填空。Choose words to fill in the blanks.

A. 下　B. 住　C. 好

① 下井必须穿 _____ 工作服。

② 他口中咬 _____ 一条毛巾。

③ 工人皮带上必须系 _____ 自救器。

④ 他从墙（qiǎng, wall）上取 _____ 一个矿灯。

语法点2 Grammar Point 2

介词：用 + 动词性成分　The preposition: 用 + verbal element
表示使用某工具做某事。
It indicates using a tool to do something.

　　Yòng bíjiā jiāzhù bíkǒng.
① 用 鼻夹夹住鼻孔。Use the nose clip to clamp the nostrils.

　　Yòng bǎohùzhào bǎohù　zìjiùqì.
② 用 保护罩保护自救器。Use the protective cover to protect the self-rescuer.

　　Yòng zuǐ hūxī.
③ 用 嘴呼吸。Use your mouth to breathe.

语法点2练习 Grammar Point Exercises 2

连词成句。Rearrange the words to form sentences.

1. ①他　　②呼吸　　③嘴　　④用　　_____
2. ①煤炭　　②他们　　③发电　　④用　　_____
3. ①煤炭职工　　②鼻夹　　③用　　④鼻孔　　⑤夹住　　_____
4. ①用　　②保护罩　　③自救器　　④保护　　⑤我们　　_____

汉字书写 Writing Chinese Characters

| dīng | 丁 丁 |
| 丁 | 丁 丁 丁 丁 |

| fāng | 方 方 方 方 |
| 方 | 方 方 方 方 |

| dǎ | 打 打 打 打 |
| 打 | 打 打 打 打 |

| fàng | 放 放 放 放 放 放 放 放 |
| 放 | 放 放 放 放 |

职业拓展 Career Insight

Disaster Avoidance in Emergency Situations

In order to perform self-rescue and mutual rescue of miners, underground workers must be familiar with and master the disaster avoidance knowledge of mines where they work in, use self-rescuers skillfully, master the signs, nature, characteristics, and disaster avoidance measures of various disasters and accidents, know about basic first-aid measures for the injured in disaster areas, and learn the most basic on-site emergency operation techniques.

小结 Summary

词语 Words

根据课文内容，选择恰当的词语。Choose the appropriate words according to the text.

1. 取下保护罩，打开 _____ 开关。

2. 拿住口具，放入口中，咬住 _____。

3. 用鼻夹夹住 _____，开始用嘴 _____。

4. 戴好 _____。

    A. 气瓶　　B. 呼吸　　C. 口具　　D. 鼻孔　　E. 安全帽

语法 Grammar

朗读下面的句子。 Read aloud the following sentences.

1. 取下自救器的保护罩。

2. 使用自救器必须咬住口具。

3. 用鼻夹夹住鼻孔。

4. 用保护罩保护自救器。

> 课文理解 Text Comprehension

根据课文内容，选词填空。Choose the words to fill in the blanks according to the text.

1. 取下保护罩，打开气瓶_____。　　A. 开关　　　B. 工作面

2. 把_____放入口中，咬住口具。　　A. 安全帽　　B. 口具

3. 用鼻夹夹住鼻孔，开始用___呼吸。　　A. 工人　　　B. 嘴

4. 煤矿职工要戴好_____。　　　　　A. 矿灯　　　B. 安全帽

第 7 课 Lesson 7

Jiǎnchá kuàngdēng
检查矿灯
Check the Miner's Lamp

 **复习 Revision**

连线。Match.

  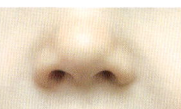  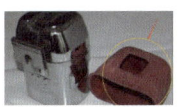 

开关　　　气瓶　　　嘴　　　鼻孔　　　呼吸　　　保护罩

 **热身 Warm-up**

下列图片你认识多少？How many of the following pictures do you know?

diànchí
电池
battery

dēngtóu
灯头
lamp cap

kuàngmào
矿帽
mining cap

pò pí
破皮
broken skin

wàiké
外壳
shell

wèntí
问题
problem

 学习生词 Words and Expressions 🎧 07-01

1	检查	jiǎnchá	v.	check
2	领取	lǐngqǔ	v.	receive
3	电池	diànchí	n.	battery
4	外壳	wàiké	n.	shell
5	有无	yǒu wú	phr.	whether
6	破损	pòsǔn	v.	damage
7	电线	diànxiàn	n.	wire
8	破皮	pò pí	phr.	broken skin
9	是否	shìfǒu	adv.	whether or not
10	明亮	míngliàng	adj.	bright
11	如果	rúguǒ	conj.	if
12	没有	méiyǒu	v.	no
13	问题	wèntí	n.	problem
14	把	bǎ	prep.	used to put the object before the verb

第7课 | 检查矿灯

15	在……上	zài……shang		on
16	灯头	dēngtóu	n.	lamp cap
17	矿帽	kuàngmào	n.	mining cap
18	有	yǒu	v.	there is, exist
19	就	jiù	adv.	*used to indicate that something comes naturally under certain conditions*
20	更换	gēnghuàn	v.	replace

词语练习 Word Exercises

1. 看图片，将相应的字母填在括号里。**Look at the pictures and fill in the corresponding letters in the brackets.**

① 外壳　（　）　② 矿帽　（　）　③ 灯头　（　）

④ 问题　（　）　⑤ 电池　（　）　⑥ 破皮　（　）

2. 朗读词语搭配。Read aloud the word collocations.

①	领取	领取矿灯	②	破损	外壳破损
		领取矿帽			矿帽破损
③	检查	检查电池	④	更换	更换电线
		检查电线			更换灯头

学习课文 Text 07-02

检查 矿灯
Jiǎnchá kuàngdēng

Gōngrén lǐngqǔ kuàngdēng hòu, jiǎnchá diànchí wàiké yǒu wú pòsǔn, diànxiàn yǒu wú pò pí, kuàngdēng shìfǒu míngliàng. Rúguǒ méiyǒu wèntí, bǎ kuàngdēng diànchí jì zài pídài shang, bǎ dēngtóu jì zài kuàngmào shang. Rúguǒ yǒu wèntí, jiù gēnghuàn kuàngdēng.

工人领取矿灯后,检查电池外壳有无破损,电线有无破皮,矿灯是否明亮。如果没有问题,把矿灯电池系在皮带上,把灯头系在矿帽上。如果有问题,就更换矿灯。

Check the Miner's Lamp

After receiving the miner's lamp, the worker shall check whether there is any damage to the battery shell, whether the wire skin is broken, and whether the lamp is bright. If there is no problem, the worker shall attach the battery of the miner's lamp to the belt and tie the lamp cap to the mining cap. If there is any problem, the worker shall replace the miner's lamp.

第7课 | 检查矿灯

课文练习 Text Exercises

1. 根据课文内容，判断对错。Tell True (T) or False (F) according to the text.

Statements	Answer
① 领取矿灯后，要检查电池外壳。	A. 是　　B. 不是
② 电池外壳破损，要更换矿灯。	A. 是　　B. 不是
③ 如果矿灯不亮，要更换矿灯。	A. 是　　B. 不是
④ 检查完矿灯后，灯头要系在腰带上。	A. 是　　B. 不是

2. 根据课文内容，选词填空。Choose the words to fill in the blanks according to the text.

① _____矿灯后，检查电池外壳有无破损。　　A. 检查　　B. 领取

② 电池外壳_____，要更换矿灯。　　A. 破损　　B. 破皮

③ 矿灯_____要系在皮带上。　　A. 电池　　B. 毛巾

④ 如果矿灯有问题，我们要_____矿灯。　　A. 破损　　B. 更换

学习语法 Grammar

语法点1 Grammar Point 1

假设复句：如果……，就…… Hypothetical complex sentences: 如果……，就……表示假设关系。第一个分句表示假设的前提，第二个分句表示能够得到的结果。It indicates a hypothetical relationship. The first clause indicates the premise of the hypothesis and the second clause indicates the result gotten.

① Rúguǒ kuàngdēng méiyǒu wèntí, jiù bǎ kuàngdēng diànchí jì zài pídài shang.
如果 矿灯 没有 问题， 就把 矿灯 电池系在皮带 上。If there is no problem with the miner's lamp, the worker shall attach the battery of the miner's lamp to the belt.

② Rúguǒ kuàngdēng yǒu wèntí, jiù gēnghuàn kuàngdēng.
如果 矿灯 有问题， 就 更换 矿灯。If there is any problem of the miner's lamp, the worker shall replace it.

③ Rúguǒ xià jǐng, jiù yào chuān gōngzuòfú, dài ānquánmào.
如果下井， 就要 穿 工作服， 戴安全帽。If the worker needs to start the downhole work, he/she needs to put on work clothes and a safety helmet.

语法点1练习 Grammar Point Exercises 1

连线，组成句子。**Match to form sentences.**

如果下井　　　　　　　　　　　　就要通过考试

如果矿灯有问题　　　　　　　　　就要取下保护罩

如果想（xiǎng, want）取得合格证　　就更换矿灯

如果使用自救器　　　　　　　　　就要戴好安全帽

语法点2 Grammar Point 2

"把"字句　"把" - Sentences

表示通过动作行为使人或事物的位置或状态发生改变。基本结构为"主语＋把＋宾语＋动词短语"。否定副词和能愿动词需放在"把"字前边。

It indicates changing the position or state of somebody or something through an action or behavior. The basic structure is "subject ＋ 把 ＋ object ＋ verbal phrase". The negative adverb or optative verb should be used before "把".

第7课 | 检查矿灯

1. Wǒmen bǎ kuàngdēng diànchí jì zài pídài shang.
   我们把矿灯电池系在皮带上。We shall attach the battery of the miner's lamp to the belt.

2. Nǐ bǎ máojīn jì zài bózi shang.
   你把毛巾系在脖子上。Tie the towel to your neck.

3. Xià jǐng shí, bìxū bǎ ānquánmào dàihǎo.
   下井时，必须把安全帽戴好。Wear the safety helmet properly when starting the downhole work.

语法点2练习 Grammar Point Exercises 2

连词成句。Rearrange the words to form sentences.

1. ①把 ②戴 ③安全帽 ④头（tóu, head）上 ⑤在

   _____

2. ①系 ②皮带上 ③在 ④把 ⑤自救器

   _____

3. ①工作服 ②把 ③胶靴 ④和 ⑤穿 ⑥好

   _____

4. ①必须 ②咬 ③口具 ④你 ⑤把 ⑥住

   _____

汉字书写 Writing Chinese Characters

huǒ 火 火 火 火
火 火 火 火 火

dìng 订 订 订 订
订 订 订 订 订

miè	灭	灭	灭	灭	灭					
灭	灭	灭	灭	灭						

dēng	灯	灯	灯	灯	灯	灯				
灯	灯	灯	灯	灯						

文化拓展 Culture Insight

The Great Wall

The Great Wall is a military defense fortification built in ancient China, which consists of tall, sturdy and continuous long walls.

The Great Wall is an ancient defense project with the longest construction duration and the biggest quantity in China and beyond. Since the Western Zhou Dynasty, it has been under construction for over 2,000 years in northern and central China, with a total length of over 20,000 kilometers.

小结 Summary

 词语 Words

朗读下面的短语。Read aloud the following phrases.

| 领取矿灯 | 更换矿灯 | 电池外壳 |
| 检查电池 | 检查电线 | 检查灯头 |

语法 Grammar

朗读下面的句子。Read aloud the following sentences.

1. 电池外壳破损。
2. 把矿灯电池系在皮带上。
3. 电线破皮。
4. 你把毛巾系在脖子上。

课文理解 Text Comprehension

根据课文内容，选词填空。Choose the words to fill in the blanks according to the text.

工人_____矿灯后，检查电池外壳有无破损，电线有无_____，矿灯是否_____。如果矿灯没有问题，把矿灯电池系在_____上，把灯头系在_____上。如果有_____，就_____矿灯。

A. 矿帽　B. 皮带　C. 问题　D. 破皮　E. 领取　F. 明亮　H. 更换

第 8 课 Lesson 8

Chéngzuò guànlóng
乘坐罐笼
Ride the Cage

 复习 Revision

连线。Match.

电线      lamp cap

问题      battery

电池      wire

灯头      shell

外壳      problem

第8课 | 乘坐罐笼

热身 Warm-up

下列图片你认识多少？ How many of the following pictures do you know?

guànlóng
罐笼
cage

chéngzuò
乘坐
ride

páiduì
排队
line up

dǎnào
打闹
be rowdy and boisterous

líkāi
离开
get out of

学习生词 Words and Expressions  08-01

1	乘坐	chéngzuò	v.	ride
2	罐笼	guànlóng	n.	cage
3	时	shí	n.	when
4	要	yào	opt.	need
5	听	tīng	v.	follow, obey
6	指挥	zhǐhuī	v.	direct
7	排队	pái//duì	v.	line up

63

8	依次	yīcì	adv.	successively
9	进入	jìnrù	v.	enter
10	最后	zuìhòu	n.	the last
11	人	rén	n.	person
12	关好	guānhǎo	phr.	close
13	门	mén	n.	door
14	当	dāng	prep.	when
15	运行	yùnxíng	v.	operate
16	站稳	zhànwěn	phr.	stand firmly
17	扶好	fúhǎo	phr.	hold tightly
18	不要	búyào	adv.	cannot
19	玩耍	wánshuǎ	v.	play
20	打闹	dǎnào	v.	be rowdy and boisterous
21	停稳	tíngwěn	phr.	stop completely
22	顺序	shùnxù	n.	order, sequence
23	离开	lí//kāi	v.	get out of, leave

词语练习 Word Exercises

1. 看图片，将相应的字母填在括号里。Look at the pictures and fill in the corresponding letters in the brackets.

第8课 | 乘坐罐笼

① 关好（　） ② 运行（　） ③ 乘坐（　） ④ 排队（　）
⑤ 门（　） ⑥ 依次（　） ⑦ 最后（　） ⑧ 罐笼（　）

2. 选词填空。Choose the words to fill in the blanks.

① 不要玩耍、（　）。  A.打闹　B.说话　C.交流

② 罐笼（　）后离开。  A.运行　B.停稳　C.移动

③ 乘坐罐笼要按（　）排好队。  A.年龄　B.大小　C.顺序

④ 乘坐罐笼要听（　）。  A.规则　B.指挥　C.时间

 学习课文　Text  08-02

Chéngzuò guànlóng
乘坐 罐笼

Chéngzuò guànlóng shí, yào tīng zhǐhuī, páiduì yīcì jìnrù,
乘坐 罐笼时，要听指挥，排队依次进入，

65

zuìhòu yí gè jìnrù de rén yào guānhǎo guànlóng de mén. Dāng guànlóng
最后一个进入的人要关好罐笼的门。当罐笼
yùnxíng shí, yào zhànwěn fúhǎo, búyào wánshuǎ, dǎnào. Guànlóng
运行时，要站稳扶好，不要玩耍、打闹。罐笼
tíngwěn hòu, àn shùnxù yīcì líkāi.
停稳后，按顺序依次离开。

Ride the Cage

When riding the cage, the workers need to follow the instructions and line up to enter it in sequence. The last person to enter the cage needs to close the door. When the cage is in operation, the workers need to stand firmly and hold the handrail tightly. Do not play or be rowdy. After the cage stops completely, get out of it in turn.

课文练习 Text Exercises

1. 根据课文内容，判断对错。Tell True(T) or False(F) according to the text.

Statements	Answer	
1 煤矿工人下井要乘坐罐笼。	A. 是	B. 不是
2 煤矿工人乘坐罐笼要听指挥。	A. 是	B. 不是
3 煤矿工人不可以在罐笼内打闹、玩耍。	A. 是	B. 不是
4 煤矿工人乘坐罐笼要关好罐笼的门。	A. 是	B. 不是

2. 根据课文内容，选词填空。Choose the words to fill in the blanks.

1 煤矿工人乘坐（　　）下井。

A. 罐笼　　　　B. 工作服　　　　C. 防护鞋

2 乘坐罐笼要关好（　　）。
　　diàntī
A. 电梯（elevator）门　　B. 罐笼门　　　　　　C. 通道

3 乘坐罐笼不可以（　　）。

A. 打闹　　　　　　B. 说话　　　　　　C. 站稳

4 乘坐罐笼后要按（　　）离开。
　　　　　　　　　　　　　dàxiǎo　　　　　　　niánlíng
A. 顺序　　　　　　B. 大小（size）　　　C. 年龄（age）

 学习语法 Grammar

 语法点1 Grammar Point 1

固定格式：（当）……时　The fixed pattern: (当)……时

用于表示在某一特定时点或时段内，在句中作状语。也可以说"当……的时候"。"……时"多用于书面语。

It is used to indicate being at a specific point in time or within a period of time and serves as an adverbial in a sentence. It is equivalent to "当……的时候" and is often used in written Chinese.

　　　Chéngzuò guànlóng shí yào páiduì yīcì jìnrù.
1 乘坐 罐笼 时要排队依次进入。When riding the cage, the workers need to line up and enter it successively.

　　　Dāng guànlóng yùnxíng shí yào zhànwěn fúhǎo.
2 当 罐笼 运行 时要 站稳 扶好。When the cage is in operation, the workers need to stand firmly and hold the handrail tightly.

　　　Gōngrén xià jǐng shí bìxū dàihǎo ānquánmào.
3 工人 下 井 时必须戴好 安全帽。When starting the downhole work, the workers must wear their safety helmets properly.

语法点 1 练习 Grammar Point Exercises 1

连线，组成句子。 Match to form sentences.

当工人下井时　　　　　要看电线有无破皮

检查矿灯时　　　　　　必须用鼻夹夹住鼻孔

使用自救器时　　　　　要坐稳扶好

当罐笼运行时　　　　　必须戴好安全帽

语法点 2 Grammar Point 2

> **能愿动词：要**　　The optative verb: 要
>
> 用在动词前，表示应该（做什么）。用于提出要求。
> It is used before a verb to indicate should (do something). It is used to make a request.
>
> ---
>
> ① Chéngzuò guànlóng shí yào tīng zhǐhuī.
> 乘坐 罐笼 时要听指挥。 When taking the cage, the workers need to follow the instructions.
>
> ② Gōngrén xià jǐng shí yào chuān gōngzuòfú.
> 工人下井时要穿工作服。 When starting the downhole work, the workers need to wear their work clothes.
>
> ③ Lǐngqǔ kuàngdēng hòu, yào jiǎnchá diànchí wàiké yǒu wú pòsǔn.
> 领取 矿灯 后，要 检查 电池 外壳 有 无 破损。 After receiving the miner's lamp, the workers need to check whether there is any damage to the battery shell.

语法点 2 练习 Grammar Point Exercises 2

用"要"完成句子。 Complete the sentences with "要".

① 乘坐罐笼时，　　　　　　② 开采煤炭时，

3. 工人下井前，_____。

4. 上中文课时，_____。

 ## 汉字书写 Writing Chinese Characters

hé
禾 禾禾禾禾禾
禾 禾禾禾禾

běi
北 北北北北北
北 北北北北

zhào
兆 兆兆兆兆兆兆
兆 兆兆兆兆

cǎi
采 采采采采采采采采
采 采采采采

 ## 职业拓展 Career Insight

Cage

Cage is a specialized equipment to transport workers up and down the mine, as well as to lift coal, gangues, materials, and equipment. It is a hub equipment to ensure normal production of the mine and safe entry and exit of workers in the mine. When the cage has been filled with materials or the mining cart has been pushed in, no one is allowed to board regardless of the quantity of materials loaded or whether there is anything inside the mining cart. For double-layer or multi-layer cages, workers and materials must be transported in layers. The layer that has been filled with materials is not allowed to be used for worker transportation.

小结 Summary

词语 Words

根据课文内容，选择恰当的词语。Choose the appropriate words according to the text.

乘坐＿＿＿＿时，要听指挥，要＿＿＿＿ ＿＿＿＿进入，最后一个进入的人要＿＿＿＿罐笼的门。

A. 排队　　　　B. 罐笼　　　　C. 关好　　　　D. 依次

语法 Grammar

朗读下面的句子。Read aloud the following sentences.

1. 当罐笼运行时，要站稳扶好。

2. 工人下井时，必须戴好安全帽。

3. 乘坐罐笼时，要听指挥。

4. 领取矿灯后，要检查电池外壳有无破损。

课文理解 Text Comprehension

根据课文内容,判断对错。Tell True (T) or False (F) according to the text.

乘坐罐笼时要听指挥。 Follow the instructions when riding the cage.	A. 是	B. 不是
最后一个进入罐笼的人要关好门。 The last person to enter the cage needs to close the door.	A. 是	B. 不是
乘坐罐笼时,要站稳扶好。 Stand firmly and hold the handrail tightly when riding the cage.	A. 是	B. 不是
乘坐罐笼时可以玩耍、打闹。 It is not allowed to play or be rowdy when riding the cage.	A. 是	B. 不是

第 9 课 Lesson 9

Chéngzuò hóuchē
乘坐猴车
Ride the Monkey Car

复习 Revision

连线。Match.

打闹　　　　　　　　　　cage

离开　　　　　　　　　　line up

罐笼　　　　　　　　　　get out of

乘坐　　　　　　　　　　be rowdy and boisterous

排队　　　　　　　　　　ride

第9课 | 乘坐猴车

 **热身 Warm-up**

下列图片你认识多少？ How many of the following pictures do you know?

hóuchē
猴车
monkey car

wèizhì
位置
position

zhuāzhù
抓住
hold

shuāng shǒu
双　手
both hands

zuòyǐ
座椅
seat

 **学习生词 Words and Expressions** 🎧 09-01

1	猴车	hóuchē	*n.*	monkey car
2	指定	zhǐdìng	*v.*	designate
3	位置	wèizhì	*n.*	position
4	双手	shuāng shǒu	*phr.*	both hands
5	抓住	zhuāzhù	*v.*	hold
6	吊杆	diàogān	*n.*	suspension rod
7	迅速	xùnsù	*adj.*	quick

73

8	坐	zuò	v.	sit
9	到	dào	v.	arrive
10	座椅	zuòyǐ	n.	seat
11	到达	dàodá	v.	reach
12	目的地	mùdìdì	n.	destination
13	双脚	shuāng jiǎo	phr.	both feet
14	踩	cǎi	v.	step on
15	地上	dìshang	n.	ground
16	座位	zuòwèi	n.	seat
17	松开	sōngkāi	phr.	loose

词语练习 Word Exercises

1. 看图片，将相应的字母填在括号里。Look at the pictures and fill in the corresponding letters in the brackets.

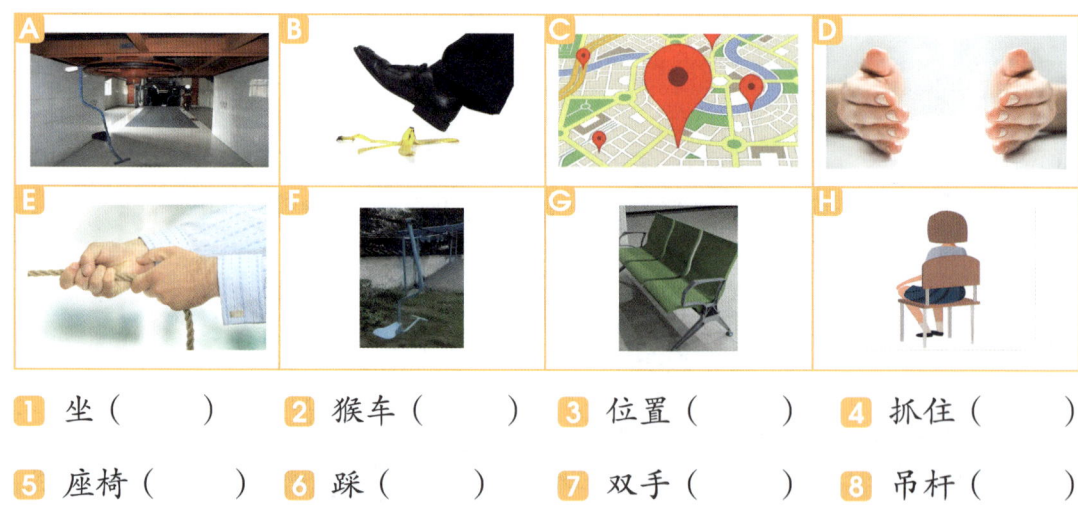

1 坐（　　）　2 猴车（　　）　3 位置（　　）　4 抓住（　　）

5 座椅（　　）　6 踩（　　）　7 双手（　　）　8 吊杆（　　）

2. 看图选词，将相应的字母填在括号里。Look at the pictures, choose the words, and fill in the corresponding letters in the brackets.

1️⃣ 离开猴车时，（　）先踩地。 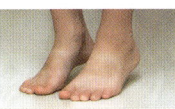 A. 双脚　B. 双手　C. 单手

2️⃣ 离开猴车时，双手（　）吊杆。  A. 抓紧　B. 松开　C. 抓住

3️⃣ 乘坐猴车时，坐在（　）上面。  A. 座椅　B. 吊杆　C. 地面

4️⃣ 到达（　）后，才可以离开猴车。  A. 巷道　B. 地面　C. 目的地

学习课文　Text　🎧 09-02

乘坐 猴车
Chéngzuò hóuchē

乘坐猴车时要排队。当猴车运行到指定位置时，双手抓住猴车的吊杆，迅速坐到猴车的座椅上，到达目的地后，双脚踩在地上，离开座位，双手松开吊杆。

Ride the Monkey Car

Line up when riding the monkey car. When the monkey car reaches the designated position, grab the suspension rod of the monkey car with both hands, quickly sit on the seats of the monkey car, step on the ground with both feet when the car reaches the destination, leave the seats and let both hands separate from the suspension rod.

课文练习 Text Exercises

1. 根据课文内容，判断对错。Tell True (T) or False (F) according to the text.

Statements	Answer
① 煤矿工人乘坐猴车要排队。	A. 是　　B. 不是
② 煤矿工人乘坐猴车时不可以抓住猴车吊杆。	A. 是　　B. 不是
③ 煤矿工人离开猴车时要双脚踩在地上。	A. 是　　B. 不是
④ 煤矿工人离开座位时需要抓住猴车吊杆。	A. 是　　B. 不是

2. 根据课文内容，选词填空。Choose the words to fill in the blanks according to the text.

① 煤矿工人下井要乘坐（　　）。

A. 安全帽　　　　B. 猴车　　　　C. 防护鞋

② 乘坐猴车要抓住（　　）。

A. 双手　　　　B. 双脚　　　　C. 吊杆

3 乘坐猴车要注意（　　　）。

A. 摇摆　　　　　B. 安全　　　　　C. 安全帽

4 离开猴车时要（　　　）踩在地上。

A. 双手　　　　　B. 双脚　　　　　C. 臀部（hip）

学习语法 Grammar

语法点 1 Grammar Point 1

动词 + 到 + 地点　Verb + 到 + place

表示动作到达终点。

It indicates the destination of a movement.

1 猴车 要 运行 到 指定 位置。The monkey car needs to reach the designated position.
（Hóuchē yào yùnxíng dào zhǐdìng wèizhì.）

2 工人 迅速 坐 到 猴车的 座椅上。The workers quickly sit on the seats of the monkey car.
（Gōngrén xùnsù zuò dào hóuchē de zuòyǐ shang.）

3 地下的 煤炭 要 运输 到 地面。Underground coal needs to be transported to the ground.
（Dìxià de méitàn yào yùnshū dào dìmiàn.）

语法点 1 练习 Grammar Point Exercises 1

连词成句。Rearrange the words to form sentences.

1 ①口具　②口中　③到　④放　⑤要

2 ①指定位置　②罐笼　③要　④到　⑤运行

_____

3 ①要　②煤炭　③运输　④地面　⑤到

_____

4 ①腰上　②要　③自救器　④系　⑤到

_____

语法点 2　Grammar Point 2

动词 + 开　Verb + 开

"开"在动词后，表示分开或离开。
"开" is used after a verb to indicate separation or departure.

1. 到达目的地后，双手松开吊杆。Let go of the suspension rod after reaching the destination.
   (Dàodá mùdìdì hòu, shuāng shǒu sōngkāi diàogān.)

2. 他推开门，进入教室。He pushed the door and entered the classroom.
   (Tā tuīkāi mén, jìnrù jiàoshì.)

3. 不要解开皮带。Do not untie the belt.
   (Búyào jiěkāi pídài.)

语法点 2 练习　Grammar Point Exercises 2

用"开""住"填空。Fill in the blanks with "开" or "住".

1 猴车运行时，双手要抓_____吊杆。　　A. 开　　B. 住

2 猴车到达目的地后，双手松_____吊杆。　　A. 开　　B. 住

3 使用自救器时，必须咬_____口具。　　A. 开　　B. 住

4 同学们推_____门，进入教室。　　A. 开　　B. 住

汉字书写 Writing Chinese Characters

文化拓展 Culture Insight

Traditional Chinese Medicine (TCM)

The basic theory of TCM is a theoretical summary of human life activities and the laws of disease changes. It mainly includes theories of *yin* and *yang*, five elements, movement and *qi*, the state of internal organs, meridians, as well as the causes, pathogenesis, diagnosis, syndrome differentiation, treatment principles, prevention, and health preservation.

Internal Canon of the Yellow Emperor has always been reputed as a classic by medical practitioners throughout history. Human beings in the vast universe may be negligible, but the influence of natural forces on humans is enormous. A person who values health preservation should learn how to comply with natural laws in the changes of the five elements and six *qi* of heaven and earth, so as to control diseases in the embryonic stage. That's why there is the saying "Superior doctor never seeks treatment for the existing sickness, but for the disease before it comes." A doctor who follows the doctrine of the mean and understands the laws of nature is called a "superior doctor". This divides the TCM (in a broad sense) into two parts in terms of application: "health preservation" and "traditional Chinese medicine". The former refers to the superior doctor who treats the disease before it comes, while the latter refers to the inferior doctor who treats the existing disease.

 小结 Summary

词语 Words

根据课文内容，选择恰当的词语。Choose the appropriate words according to the text.

当_____运行到指定_____时，双手_____猴车的吊杆，_____坐到猴车的座椅上。

  A. 迅速   B. 猴车   C. 位置   D. 抓住

语法 Grammar

朗读下面的句子。Read aloud the following sentences.

1. 猴车要运行到指定位置。
2. 到达目的地后，双手松开吊杆。
3. 工人迅速坐到猴车的座椅上。
4. 他推开门，进入教室。

课文理解 Text Comprehension

根据课文内容，判断对错。Tell True (T) or False (F) according to the text.

乘坐猴车时要排队。 Line up when riding the monkey car.	A. 是　　B. 不是
乘坐猴车时要迅速抓住吊杆。 Quickly hold the suspension rod when riding the monkey car.	A. 是　　B. 不是
猴车运行到指定位置时才可以乘坐。 Don't get on the monkey car until it reaches the designated position.	A. 是　　B. 不是
乘坐猴车时要迅速坐到座椅上。 Quickly sit on the seat of the monkey car when riding the monkey car.	A. 是　　B. 不是

第10课 / lesson 10

Jǐngxià xíngzǒu
井下行走
Walk During Downhole Work

 复习 Revision

连线。 Match.

抓住		monkey car
座椅		position
猴车		seat
位置		both hands
双手		hold

第 10 课 | 井下行走

 **热身 Warm-up**

下列图片你认识多少？ How many of the following pictures do you know?

lùbiāo
路标
road sign

xíngzǒu
行走
walk

rénxíngdào
人行道
sidewalk

jìnzhǐ rù nèi
禁止入内
no entry

zhùyì
注意
notice

jǐnggào biāozhì
警告 标志
warning sign

hàngdào
巷道
tunnel

chēliàng
车辆
vehicle

xìnhàodēng
信号灯
signal lamp

 **学习生词 Words and Expressions** 🎧 10-01

1	行走	xíngzǒu	*v.*	walk
2	应	yīng	*opt.*	should
3	拿	ná	*v.*	take

83

4	携带	xiédài	v.	carry
5	物品	wùpǐn	n.	object
6	走	zǒu	v.	walk
7	人行道	rénxíngdào	n.	sidewalk
8	不得	bùdé	opt.	not be allowed
9	注意	zhùyì	v.	notice
10	里	li	n.	in
11	信号灯	xìnhàodēng	n.	signal lamp
12	车辆	chēliàng	n.	vehicle
13	路标	lùbiāo	n.	road sign
14	挂	guà	v.	hang
15	禁止入内	jìnzhǐ rù nèi	phr.	no entry
16	警告标志	jǐnggào biāozhì	phr.	warning sign

词语练习　Word Exercises

1. 看图片，将相应的字母填在括号里。Look at the pictures and fill in the corresponding letters in the brackets.

第 10 课 | 井下行走

❶ 巷道（   ）　　❷ 禁止入内（   ）　　❸ 行走（   ）

❹ 车辆（   ）　　❺ 信号灯（   ）　　❻ 路标（   ）

2. 朗读词语搭配。Read aloud the word collocations.

❶ 注意	注意信号灯	❷ 进入	进入人行道
	注意路标		进入巷道
❸ 禁止	禁止行走	❹ 携带	携带矿灯
	禁止入内		携带毛巾

 学习课文　Text　🔊 10-02

井下行走
Jǐngxià xíngzǒu

井下行走时，应拿好携带的物品，走人行道。不得取下安全帽和矿灯。要注意巷道里的信号灯、车辆和路标。不得进入挂有"禁止入内"警告标志的巷道。

Walk During Downhole Work

When walking during downhole work, take your belongings and walk on the sidewalk. Do not remove your safety helmet or miner's lamp. Notice the signal lamps, vehicles, and road signs in the tunnel. Do not enter the tunnel hanging with the warning sign of "No Entry".

课文练习 Text Exercises

1. 根据课文内容，判断对错。Tell True (T) or False (F) according to the text.

Statements	Answer
❶ 在井下行走时应走人行道。	A. 是　　B. 不是
❷ 可以进入挂有"禁止入内"警告标志的巷道。	A. 是　　B. 不是
❸ 在井下行走时可以取下安全帽。	A. 是　　B. 不是
❹ 在井下行走时要拿好携带的物品。	A. 是　　B. 不是

2. 根据课文内容，选词填空。Choose the words to fill in the blanks according to the text.

❶ 在井下行走时，我们要注意（　　）。

A. 信号灯　　　　　　　　B. 安全帽　　　　C. 矿灯

❷ 在井下行走时，应走（　　）。

A. 路标　　　　　　　　　B. 人行道　　　　C. 矿灯

❸ 进入矿井工作前，要（　　）。

A. 戴安全帽　　　　　　　B. 注意信号灯　　C. 人行道

❹ 在矿井下行走时，不得进入（　　）。

A. 挂有"禁止入内"标志的巷道　　B. 人行道　　C. 巷道

第10课 | 井下行走

 学习语法 Grammar

 语法点1 Grammar Point 1

能愿动词：应　The optative verb: 应

表示理所当然。多用于书面语。口语中多用"应该"。

It indicates being supposed to do something as a matter of course. It is often used in written Chinese and "应该" (should) is often used in spoken Chinese.

1. Jǐngxià xíngzǒu shí, yīng náhǎo xiédài de wùpǐn.
   井下行走时，应拿好携带的物品。Take your belongings with you when walking during downhole work.

2. Jǐngxià xíngzǒu shí, yīng zǒu rénxíngdào.
   井下行走时，应走人行道。Use the sidewalk when walking during downhole work.

3. Jǐngxià xíngzǒu shí, yīng dàihǎo ānquánmào.
   井下行走时，应戴好安全帽。Wear your safety helmet when walking during downhole work.

语法点1练习 Grammar Point Exercises 1

用"应"完成句子。Complete the sentences with "应".

1. 井下行走时，_____。

2. 准备下井前，_____。

3. 领取矿灯后，_____。

4. 乘坐罐笼时，_____。

87

语法点 2 Grammar Point 2

能愿动词：不得　The optative verb: 不得

用在动词前，表示禁止、不许可。
It is used before a verb to indicate prohibition or disapproval.

1. Jǐngxià xíngzǒu shí, bùdé qǔxia ānquánmào hé kuàngdēng.
   井下 行走 时，不得取下 安全帽 和 矿灯。Do not remove your safety helmet or miner's lamp when walking during downhole.

2. Bùdé jìnrù guàyǒu "jìnzhǐ rù nèi" biāozhì de hàngdào.
   不得进入挂有"禁止入内"标志的巷道。Do not enter the tunnel hanging with the warning sign of "No Entry".

3. Chéngzuò hóuchē shí, bùdé líkāi zuòwèi.
   乘坐 猴车 时，不得离开座位。Do not leave your seat when taking the monkey car.

语法点 2 练习 Grammar Point Exercises 1

用"不得"完成句子。Complete the sentences with "不得".

1. 井下行走时，_____。
2. 乘坐罐笼时，_____。
3. 乘坐猴车时，_____。
4. 使用自救器时，_____。

汉字书写 Writing Chinese Characters

rén
人 人
人 人 人 人 人

职业拓展 Career Insight

Downhole Work Preparations

Before the downhole work, the workers need to prepare the miner's lamps and the self-rescuers, and then check the self-rescuers. During the downhole work, to avoid accidents caused by electric sparks, they cannot strike the lamp box or the lamp cap and open the lamp cap or the battery box cover.

小结 Summary

词语 Words

根据课文内容，选择恰当的词语。Choose the appropriate words according to the text.

　　井下行走时，应拿好携带的物品，走_____。不得取下_____和矿灯。要注意巷道里的_____、车辆和路标。不得进入挂有"_____"

警告标志的巷道。

A. 安全帽　　　B. 禁止入内　　　C. 人行道　　　D. 信号灯

语法 Grammar

朗读下面的句子。 Read aloud the following sentences.

1. 井下行走时，应拿好携带的物品。

2. 井下行走时，应走人行道。

3. 井下行走时，不得取下安全帽和矿灯。

4. 不得进入挂有"禁止入内"标志的巷道。

课文理解 Text Comprehension

根据课文内容，判断对错。Tell True (T) or False (F) according to the text.

在井下行走时，要戴好安全帽和矿灯。 Wear your safety helmet and miner's lamp when walking during downhole work.	A. 是	B. 不是
井下行走时，可以玩耍、打闹。 Playing or being rowdy is allowed when walking during downhole work.	A. 是	B. 不是
在井下行走时，我们应走人行道。 Use the sidewalk when walking during downhole work.	A. 是	B. 不是
在井下行走时，我们要注意车辆。 Watch out for vehicles when walking during downhole work.	A. 是	B. 不是

第 11 课 lesson 11

Tōngguò fēngmén
通过风门
Pass Through the Damper

 ## 复习 Revision

连线。 Match.

巷道　车辆　路标　禁止入内　人行道　信号灯

 ## 热身 Warm-up

下列图片你认识多少？ How many of the following pictures do you know?

fēngmén guānbì　　　　fēngmén dǎkāi　　　　yánjìn
风门 关闭　　　　　　风门 打开　　　　　　严禁
damper closed　　　　　damper opened　　　　strictly prohibit

职通中文 煤矿开采技术（初级篇）

rényuán
人员
personnel

liǎng
两
two, both

tóngshí dǎkāi
同时打开
open simultaneously

学习生词 Words and Expressions 🎧 11-01

1	风门	fēngmén	n.	damper
2	先	xiān	adv.	first
3	道	dào	m.	a measure word for doors
4	所有	suǒyǒu	adj.	all
5	人员	rényuán	n.	personnel
6	立即	lìjí	adv.	immediately
7	关上	guānshang	phr.	close
8	然后	ránhòu	conj.	then
9	另	lìng	pron.	the other
10	待	dài	v.	wait for
11	严禁	yánjìn	v.	strictly prohibit
12	两	liǎng	num.	two, both
13	同时	tóngshí	n.	simultaneously

第 11 课 | 通过风门

词语练习 Word Exercises

1. 看图片，将相应的字母填在括号里。Look at the pictures and fill in the corresponding letters in the brackets.

  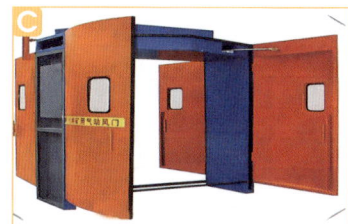

❶ 人员　　　（　　）　❷ 两　　　　（　　）　❸ 风门 打开　（　　）

❹ 同时打开　（　　）　❺ 风门 关闭　（　　）　❻ 严禁　　　（　　）

2. 朗读词语搭配。Read aloud the word collocations.

❶ 打开	打开风门	❷ 关上	关上风门
	打开矿灯		关上开关
❸ 严禁	严禁两道风门同时打开	❹ 通过	通过巷道
	严禁烟火（yānhuǒ, firework）		通过人行道

学习课文 Text 🎧 11-02

通过风门
Tōngguò fēngmén

通过风门时，先打开一道风门，所有人员进入后，立即关上风门，然后打开另一道风门，待所有人员通过后，必须把风门关好。严禁两道风门同时打开。

Pass Through the Damper

When passing through the damper, first open a damper. After all the personnel have entered, close the damper immediately, and then open the other damper. After all the personnel have passed through, close the damper tightly. It is strictly prohibited to open both dampers simultaneously.

课文练习 Text Exercises

1. 根据课文内容，判断对错。Tell True (T) or False (F) according to the text.

Statements	Answer
① 通过风门时，可以同时打开两道风门。	A. 是　　B. 不是
② 所有人员通过风门后，必须把风门关好。	A. 是　　B. 不是

3 通过风门时，先打开一道风门，待所有人员进入后立即关上风门，然后打开另一道风门。	A. 是	B. 不是
4 通过风门时，先打开一道风门，待所有人员进入后打开另一道风门。	A. 是	B. 不是

2. 根据课文内容，选词填空。Choose the words to fill in the blanks according to the text.

1 通过风门时，先打开（　　）风门。

　A. 一道　　　　B. 两道　　　　　C. 三道

2 所有人员通过风门后，必须把风门（　　）。

　A. 打开　　　　B. 关上　　　　　C. 打开或关上都行

3 所有人员进入一道风门后，应（　　）。

　A. 立即关上风门，然后打开另一道风门

　B. 同时打开另一道风门　　　C. 都（dōu）（both, all）可以

4 通过风门时，（　　）同时打开两道风门。

　A. 可以　　　　B. 严禁　　　　　C. 必须

学习语法 Grammar

语法点 1 Grammar Point 1

先……然后……
表示两个动作行为的先后顺序。
It indicates the sequence of two actions.

① 通过风门时先打开一道风门,所有人员进入后,立即关上风门。然后打开另一道风门。When passing through the damper, first open an damper, and immediately close it after all personnel have entered. Then open another damper.

② 下井前先穿好工作服、戴好安全帽、检查好矿灯和自救器,然后乘坐罐笼下井。Before going down the shaft, put on work clothes, wear a safety helmet, check the mining lamp and self-rescuer, and then take the cage to go down the shaft.

③ 使用矿灯时先检查电池外壳和电线有无破损、矿灯是否明亮,然后把矿灯电池系在皮带上,把灯头系在矿帽上。When using the miner's lamp, first check whether the battery shell and wires are damaged, whether the miner's lamp is bright, and then tie the battery of the miner's lamp to the belt and the lamp cap to the miner's cap.

语法点1练习 Grammar Point Exercises 1

用"先……,然后……"改写句子。Rewrite the sentences with "先……,然后……".

① 打开一道风门,打开另一道风门。

② 穿好工作服和胶靴,戴好安全帽。

③ 系好矿灯和自救器,乘坐罐笼下井。

④ 检查矿灯有无损坏,把灯头系在矿帽上。

语法点 2 Grammar Point 2

形容词：所有 The adjective: 所有

表示全部、没有例外。常用结构为"所有（的）+ 名词"。
It indicates "all, no exception". The common structure is "所有 (的) + noun".

1. Suǒyǒu gōngrén jìnrù hòu, lìjí guānshang fēngmén.
   所有 工人 进入后，立即 关上 风门。After all the workers have entered, immediately close the damper.

2. Dài suǒyǒu rényuán tōngguò hòu, bìxū bǎ fēngmén guānhǎo.
   待 所有 人员 通过 后，必须把 风门 关好。After all the personnel have passed through, the damper must be closed properly.

3. Xià jǐng qián yào zuòhǎo suǒyǒu de zhǔnbèi gōngzuò.
   下井 前 要 做好 所有的 准备 工作。Make all the necessary preparations before going down the shaft.

语法点 2 练习 Grammar Point Exercises 2

连词成句。Rearrange the words to form sentences.

1. ①职工　②所有　③必须　④安全　⑤参加　⑥培训

   _____

2. ①我们　②检查　③要　④设备　⑤所有

   _____

3. ①行走　②井下　③应　④拿好　⑤物品　⑥所有　⑦时

   _____

4. ①所有的　②下井前　③要　④学习　⑤知识　⑥安全

   _____

汉字书写 Writing Chinese Characters

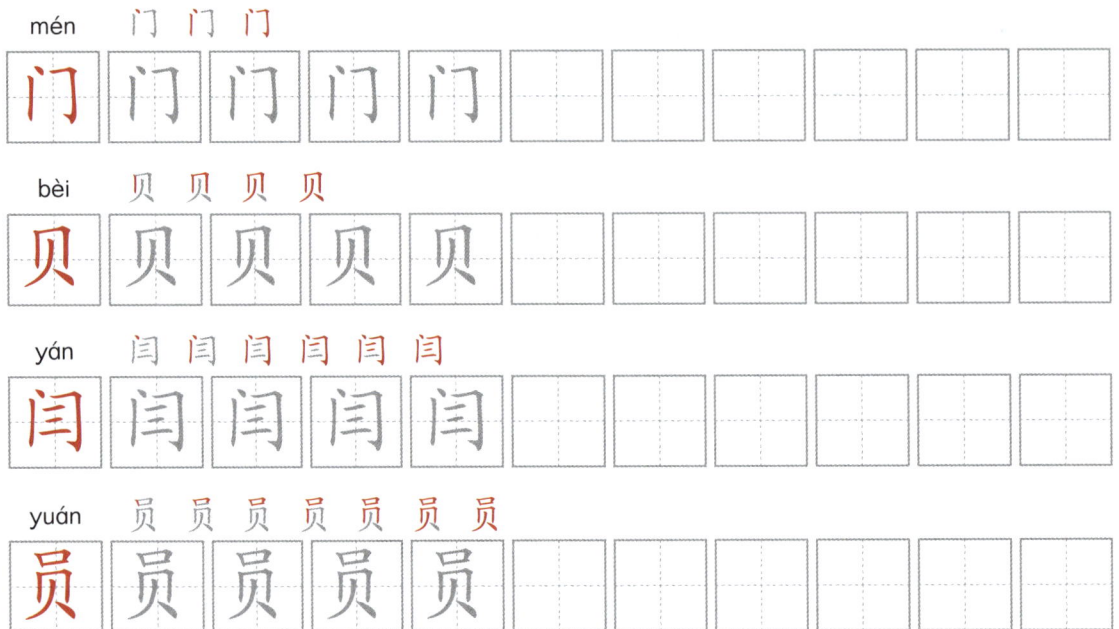

文化拓展 Culture Insight

Beijing Opera

Beijing opera is one of the Chinese treasures and is the most influential opera type in China. It is based in Beijing and is popularized in various parts of the country. Beijing opera is an important expression form of traditional Chinese culture, and its artistic elements are likened to symbolic symbols of traditional Chinese culture. In 2010, Beijing opera was listed in The Representative List of the Intangible Cultural Heritage of Humanity of the UNESCO Intangible Cultural Heritage List.

第 11 课 | 通过风门

 小结 Summary

词语 Words

根据课文内容，选择恰当的词语。Choose the appropriate words according to the text.

1. 先打开一道风门，待所有人员进入后，立即关上（　　）。

    A. 矿灯　B. 风门

2. 先检查电池外壳和电线有无破损，矿灯是否（　　）。

    A. 损坏　B. 破皮

3. 严禁两道风门（　　）打开。

    A. 同时　B. 然后

4. （　　）人员通过后，必须把风门关好。

    A. 所有　B. 一个

语法 Grammar

朗读下面的句子。Read aloud the following sentences.

1. 通过风门时，先打开一道风门，所有人员进入后，立即关上风门，然后打开另一道风门。

2. 下井前，先穿好工作服、戴好安全帽、检查好矿灯和自救器，然后乘坐罐笼下井。

3 所有工人进入后,立即关上风门。

4 待所有人员通过后,必须把风门关好。

课文理解 Text Comprehension

复述课文内容。Retell the text.

通过风门时,先_____一道风门,_____人员进入后,_____关上风门,_____打开另一道风门,_____所有人员通过后,_____把风门关好。_____两道风门_____打开。

第 12 课 Lesson 12

Jiǎnchá wǎjiǎnyí guānglù
检查瓦检仪光路
Check the Light Path of the Gas Detector

复习 Revision

连线。 Match.

风门关闭　　　　　　strictly prohibit

人员　　　　　　two, both

两　　　　　　damper opened

严禁　　　　　　open simultaneously

同时打开　　　　　　personnel

风门打开　　　　　　damper closed

 ## 热身 Warm-up

下列图片你认识多少? How many of the following pictures do you know?

guāngyuán
光 源
light source

ànniǔ
按 钮
button

mùjìng
目 镜
eyepiece

fēnhuábǎn
分划板
reticle

gānshè tiáowén
干涉 条纹
interference fringe

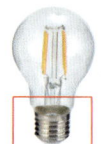
dēngpào hòugài
灯泡 后盖
rear cover of the bulb

 ## 学习生词 Words and Expressions  12-01

1	瓦检仪	wǎjiǎnyí	n.	gas detector
2	光路	guānglù	n.	light path
3	按	àn	v.	press
4	光源	guāngyuán	n.	light source
5	按钮	ànniǔ	n.	button
6	目镜	mùjìng	n.	eyepiece
7	观察	guānchá	v.	observe
8	分划板	fēnhuábǎn	n.	reticle

9	清晰	qīngxī	*adj.*	clear
10	旋转	xuánzhuǎn	*v.*	rotate
11	调整	tiáozhěng	*v.*	adjust
12	度	dù	*suf.*	degree
13	干涉条纹	gānshè tiáowén	*phr.*	interference fringe
14	拧松	nǐngsōng	*phr.*	unscrew
15	后盖	hòugài	*n.*	rear cover

词语练习 Word Exercises

1. 看图片，将相应的字母填在括号里。Look at the pictures and fill in the corresponding letters in the brackets.

❶ 光源　　　　（　） ❷ 灯泡后盖　（　） ❸ 分划板　　（　）

❹ 干涉条纹　（　） ❺ 目镜　　　（　） ❻ 按钮　　　（　）

2. 朗读词语搭配。Read aloud the word collocations.

❶	观察	观察按钮	❷ 按下	按下按钮
		观察干涉条纹		按下开关
❸	调整	调整目镜	❹ 旋转	旋转目镜
		调整灯泡后盖		旋转按钮

学习课文 Text 🎧 12-02

检查瓦检仪光路
Jiǎnchá wǎjiǎnyí guānglù

1. 按下光源按钮,通过目镜观察分划板是否清晰。
   Ànxià guāngyuán ànniǔ, tōngguò mùjìng guānchá fēnhuábǎn shìfǒu qīngxī.

2. 旋转目镜,调整分划板清晰度。
   Xuánzhuǎn mùjìng, tiáozhěng fēnhuábǎn qīngxīdù.

3. 观察干涉条纹是否清晰。
   Guānchá gānshè tiáowén shìfǒu qīngxī.

4. 拧松灯泡后盖,调整干涉条纹清晰度。
   Nǐngsōng dēngpào hòugài, tiáozhěng gānshè tiáowén qīngxīdù.

Check the Light Path of the Gas Detector

1. Press the light source button and observe through the eyepiece to see whether the reticle is clear.

2. Rotate the eyepiece and adjust the clearness degree of the reticle.

3. Observe whether the interference fringes are clear.

4. Unscrew the rear cover of the bulb and adjust the clearness degree of the interference fringes.

课文练习 Text Exercises

1. 根据课文内容，判断对错。Tell True (T) or False (F) according to the text.

Statements	Answer
❶ 检查瓦检仪光路时，通过目镜观察分划板是否清晰。	A. 是　　B. 不是
❷ 通过旋转目镜，可以调整分划板清晰度。	A. 是　　B. 不是
❸ 干涉条纹清晰度不可以调整。	A. 是　　B. 不是
❹ 通过目镜观察分划板清晰度时，要按下光源按钮。	A. 是　　B. 不是

2. 根据课文内容，选词填空。Choose the words to fill in the blanks according to the text.

❶ 检查瓦检仪光路时，通过（　　）观察分划板是否清晰。

A. 灯泡　　　　B. 目镜　　　　C. 光源

❷ 通过旋转目镜，（　　）调整分划板清晰度。

A. 可以　　　　B. 不可以　　　C. 不要

❸ 干涉条纹不清晰，可以通过（　　）灯泡后盖调整干涉条纹清晰度。

A. 按下　　　　B. 观察　　　　C. 拧松

❹ （　　）目镜，调整分划板清晰度。

A. 打开　　　　B. 关上　　　　C. 旋转

学习语法 Grammar

语法点 1 Grammar Point 1

介词：通过　The preposition: 通过

用于引出行为的媒介或手段。常用结构为"通过……+ 动词性词语"。
It is used to introduce the medium or method of a behavior. The common structure is "通过 …… + verbal phrase".

1. Tōngguò mùjìng guānchá fēnhuàbǎn shìfǒu qīngxī.
通过 目镜 观察 分划板 是否 清晰。Observe the reticle through the eyepiece to see if it is clear.

2. Tōngguò xuánzhuǎn mùjìng tiáozhěng fēnhuàbǎn qīngxīdù.
通过 旋转 目镜 调整 分划板 清晰度。Adjust the clearness degree of the reticle by rotating the eyepiece.

3. Tōngguò nǐngsōng dēngpào hòugài tiáozhěng gānshè tiáowén qīngxīdù.
通过 拧松 灯泡 后盖 调整 干涉 条纹 清晰度。Adjust the clearness degree of interference fringes by loosening the back cover of the bulb.

语法点 1 练习 Grammar Point Exercises 1

连线。Match.

1. 通过旋转目镜　　　　　　发电
2. 通过参加安全培训　　　　运输煤炭
3. 通过开掘巷道　　　　　　调整分划板清晰度
4. 通过燃烧煤炭　　　　　　学习井下应急措施

语法点 2 Grammar Point 2

副词：是否 The adverb: 是否

意思是"是不是"，多用于书面语。常用结构为"主语 + 是否 + 谓语"。

It means "whether" and is often used in written Chinese. The common structure is "subject + 是否 + predicate".

1. 观察 分划板 是否 清晰。Observe whether the reticle is clear.
   Guānchá fēnhuábǎn shìfǒu qīngxī.

2. 观察 干涉 条纹 是否 清晰。Observe whether the interference fringes are clear.
   Guānchá gānshè tiáowén shìfǒu qīngxī.

3. 检查 矿灯 电池 是否 有 破损。Check if the battery of the miner's lamp is damaged.
   Jiǎnchá kuàngdēng diànchí shìfǒu yǒu pòsǔn.

语法点 2 练习 Grammar Point Exercises 2

连词成句。Rearrange the words to form sentences.

1. ①检查 ②是否 ③破皮 ④有 ⑤电线

   _____

2. ①职工 ②取得 ③要 ④是否 ⑤合格证

   _____

3. ①是否 ②工人 ③通过 ④可以 ⑤考试

   _____

4. ①干涉条纹 ②是否 ③观察 ④清晰

   _____

汉字书写 Writing Chinese Characters

职业拓展 Career Insight

Learn the Optical Gas Detector

Optical gas detector, abbreviated as gas detector, is an instrument used underground in coal mines to measure the concentrations of gas and carbon dioxide. According to its measurement range of gas concentration, it is divided into two types: 0%-10% type (accuracy 0.01%) and 0%-100% type (accuracy 0.1%). Its features include high portability, easy operation, safety and high accuracy, but it has a complex structure and high maintenance costs.

第12课 | 检查瓦检仪光路

小结 Summary

 词语 Words

根据课文内容，选择恰当的词语。Choose the appropriate words according to the text.

1. 检查瓦检仪（　　）时，通过目镜观察分划板是否清晰。

   A. 电路　　　　B. 光路　　　　C. 药品

2. 通过（　　）目镜，可以调整分划板清晰度。

   A. 打开　　　　B. 关上　　　　C. 旋转

3. （　　）不清晰，可以通过拧松灯泡后盖调整它的清晰度。

   A. 干涉条纹　　B. 目镜　　　　C. 分划板

4. 按下光源（　　），通过目镜观察分划板是否清晰。

   A. 按钮　　　　B. 后盖　　　　C. 灯泡

语法 Grammar

朗读下面的句子。Read aloud the following sentences.

1. 通过目镜观察分划板是否清晰。
2. 通过旋转目镜调整分划板清晰度。
3. 观察分划板是否清晰。
4. 观察干涉条纹是否清晰。

> **课文理解** Text Comprehension

复述课文内容。Retell the text.

　　检查瓦检仪光路时，要按下光源_____，通过_____观察分划板是否_____。旋转_____，调整分划板_____。观察_____是否清晰。拧松_____后盖，_____干涉条纹清晰度。

第 13 课 Lesson 13

Jiǎnchá wǎjiǎnyí qìmìxìng
检查瓦检仪气密性
Check the Airtightness of the Gas Detector

 复习 Revision

连线。Match.

干涉条纹　　　　　　button

按钮　　　　　　eyepiece

分划板　　　　　　interference fringe

目镜　　　　　　reticle

111

 **热身 Warm-up**

下列图片你认识多少？ How many of the following pictures do you know?

xīqìqiú
吸气球
suction balloon

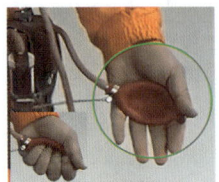
niēbiǎn
捏扁
squeeze sth. flat

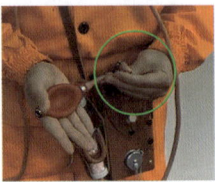
qiāzhù
掐住
pinch

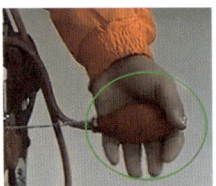
zhàngqǐ
胀起
bulge

jiāoguǎn
胶管
rubber hose

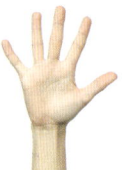
shǒu
手
hand

 **学习生词 Words and Expressions**  13-01

1	气密性	qìmìxìng	n.	airtightness
2	捏扁	niēbiǎn	phr.	squeeze sth. flat
3	吸气球	xīqìqiú	n.	suction balloon
4	掐住	qiāzhù	phr.	pinch
5	胶管	jiāoguǎn	n.	rubber hose
6	如果……就……	rúguǒ……jiù……		if...then...
7	胀起	zhàngqǐ	phr.	bulge

第 13 课 ｜ 检查瓦检仪气密性

8	表明	biǎomíng	v.	indicate
9	漏气	lòu qì	phr.	air leakage
10	进气孔	jìnqìkǒng	n.	air inlet
11	再	zài	adv.	then
12	恢复	huīfù	v.	recover
13	气路	qìlù	n.	air path
14	畅通	chàngtōng	adj.	unblocked

词语练习 Word Exercises

1. 看图片，将相应的字母填在括号里。Look at the pictures and fill in the corresponding letters in the brackets.

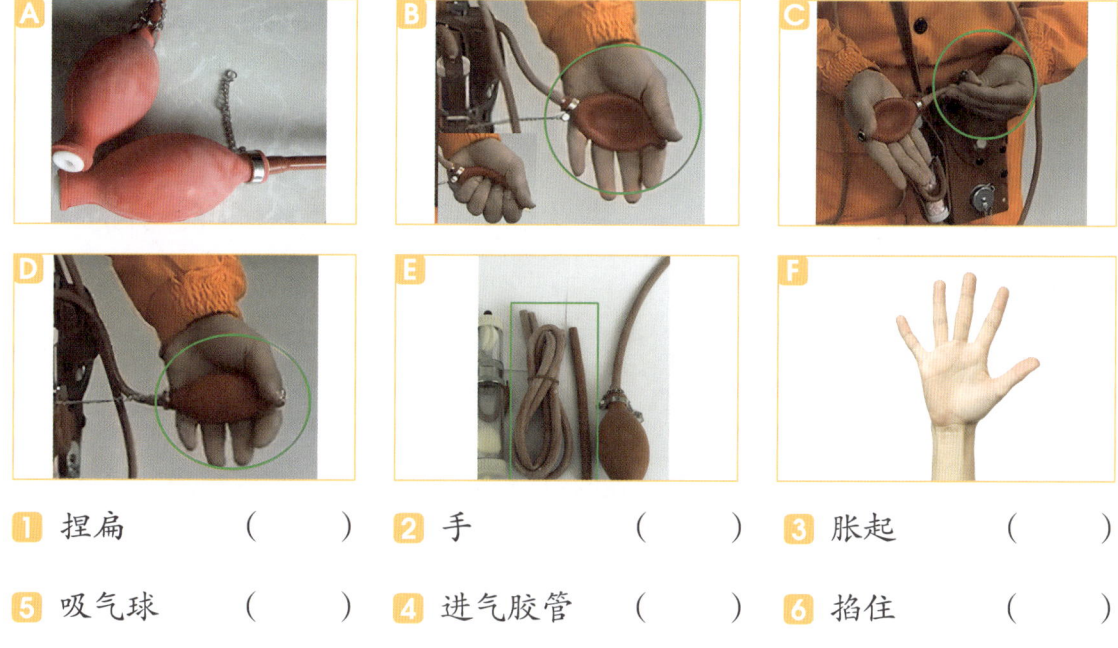

1 捏扁　　（　） 2 手　　　　　（　） 3 胀起　（　）

5 吸气球　（　） 4 进气胶管　（　） 6 掐住　（　）

2. 朗读词语搭配。Read aloud the word collocations.

① 捏扁	捏扁吸气球	② 松开	松开吸气球
	捏扁水瓶		松开安全帽系带
③ 掐住	掐住胶管	④ 用	用安全帽
	掐住手指		用矿灯

 学习课文 Text 🎧 13-02

检查瓦检仪气密性
Jiǎnchá wǎjiǎnyí qìmìxìng

1. 先用一只手捏扁吸气球，另一只手掐住胶管，然后松开吸气球，如果吸气球不胀起，就表明不漏气。

2. 放开进气孔，先捏扁吸气球，再放开。如果吸气球可以恢复，就表明气路畅通。

Check the Airtightness of the Gas Detector

1. First, squeeze the suction balloon with one hand to flatten it, pinch the rubber hose with the other hand, and then release the suction balloon. If the balloon does not bulge, it indicates that there is no air leakage.

第13课 | 检查瓦检仪气密性

2. Open the air inlet, first squeeze the suction balloon to flatten it, and then release it. If the balloon can recover, it indicates that the air path is unblocked.

课文练习 Text Exercises

1. 根据课文内容，判断对错。Tell True (T) or False (F) according to the text.

Statements	Answer	
① 检查瓦检仪气密性时，直接观察吸气球，如果吸气球胀起，就表明不漏气。	A. 是	B. 不是
② 用一只手先捏扁吸气球，然后松开吸气球，如果吸气球不胀起，就表明不漏气。	A. 是	B. 不是
③ 用一只手捏扁吸气球，另一只手必须掐住胶管，然后松开吸气球，如果吸气球不胀起，就表明不漏气。	A. 是	B. 不是
④ 放开进气孔，如果吸气球可以恢复，就表明气路畅通。	A. 是	B. 不是

2. 根据课文内容，选词填空。Choose the words to fill in the blanks according to the text.

① 检查瓦检仪气密性时，先用手（　　）吸气球。

A. 掐住　　　　B. 捏扁　　　　C. 拿上

② 用手捏扁吸气球，另一手掐住（　　），然后松开吸气球，观察吸气球是否漏气。

A. 吸气球　　　B. 进气孔　　　C. 胶管

115

3 放开进气孔，捏扁再放开吸气球，如果吸气球能恢复，就表明（　　）畅通。

 A. 电路　　　　B. 光路　　　　C. 气路

4 如果吸气球（　　），就表明不漏气。

 A. 恢复　　　　B. 不胀起　　　C. 不变化

学习语法 Grammar

 语法点1 Grammar Point 1

如果……，就……

表示假设关系。第一个分句表示假设的前提，第二个分句表示在第一个分句的前提下能够得到的结果。

It indicates a hypothetical relationship. The first clause indicates the premise of the hypothesis, and the second clause indicates the result under the premise of the first clause.

---

1 Rúguǒ xīqìqiú bú zhàngqǐ, jiù biǎomíng bú lòu qì.
如果吸气球不胀起，就表明不漏气。If the balloon does not bulge, it indicates that there is no air leakage.

2 Rúguǒ xīqìqiú kěyǐ huīfù, jiù biǎomíng qìlù chàngtōng.
如果吸气球可以恢复，就表明气路畅通。If the balloon can recover, it shows that the air path is unblocked.

3 Rúguǒ kuàngdēng diànchí wàiké pòsǔn, jiù yào gēnghuàn kuàngdēng.
如果矿灯电池外壳破损，就要更换矿灯。If the battery shell of the miner's lamp is damaged, the miner's lamp needs to be replaced.

第 13 课 ｜ 检查瓦检仪气密性

语法点 1 练习 Grammar Point Exercises 1

连线。 Match.

如果分划板不清晰　　　　就表明气路不通畅

如果矿灯没有问题　　　　就可以通过目镜调整

如果在井下行走　　　　　就要注意车辆和路标

如果吸气球不恢复　　　　就把灯头系在矿帽上

语法点 2 Grammar Point 2

先……，再……

表示两个动作行为在时间上连续进行，含有强调先后顺序不能改变的意思，后一动作在前一动作完成后做。

It indicates that two actions are consecutively performed in time, emphasizing that the order cannot be changed, and the latter action is performed after the completion of the previous action.

1. Xiān qiāzhù jiāoguǎn, zài sōngkāi xīqìqiú.
先 掐住 胶管，再 松开 吸气球。Pinch the rubber hose first, then release the suction balloon.

2. Xiān dàihǎo ānquánmào, zài chéngzuò guànlóng xià jǐng.
先 戴好 安全帽，再 乘坐 罐笼 下井。Wear a safety helmet first, and then ride the cage down the shaft.

3. Xiān guānshang yí dào fēngmén, zài dǎkāi lìng yí dào fēngmén.
先 关上 一道 风门，再打开另一道 风门。Close an damper first, then open another damper.

语法点 2 练习 Grammar Point Exercises 2

用"先……再……"完成句子。Complete the sentences with "先 …… 再 ……".

1. 工人要先参加安全培训，_____。

117

2. 领取矿灯后，要先_____，再_____。

3. 准备下井时，要先_____，再_____。

4. 检查瓦检仪光路时，要先按下光源按钮，再_____。

 汉字书写 Writing Chinese Characters

 文化拓展 Culture Insight

Giant Panda

Giant pandas belong to the Ursidae family and are mammals. Their black and white appearances help them hide in dense forests and snow-covered ground, reducing the probability to be detected by their natural enemies. Giant pandas have been living on the earth for at least 8 million years and are known as "living fossils" and "China's national treasures". As the ambassador of the World

Wildlife Fund, they are also seen as the flagship species of global biodiversity conservation. Giant pandas are unique to China, and they mainly inhabit in mountainous areas of Sichuan, Shaanxi, and Gansu provinces in China.

小结 Summary

词语 Words

朗读下面的短语。Read aloud the following phrases.

1. 捏扁吸气球　　吸气球胀起
2. 松开吸气球　　吸气球漏气
3. 放开进气孔　　吸气球恢复
4. 掐住胶管　　　气路通畅

语法 Grammar

朗读下面的句子。Read aloud the following sentences.

1. 如果吸气球不胀起，就表明不漏气。
2. 如果吸气球可以恢复，就表明气路畅通。
3. 先掐住胶管，再松开吸气球。
4. 先戴好安全帽，再乘坐罐笼下井。

课文理解 Text Comprehension

复述课文内容。Retell the text.

　　检查瓦检仪气密性时，要先用一只手_____吸气球，另一只手掐住_____，然后松开_____，如果吸气球不胀起，就表明不_____。放开进气孔，先捏扁_____，再放开。如果吸气球可以_____，就表明气路_____。

第 14 课 Lesson 14

检查瓦检仪药品
Jiǎnchá wǎjiǎnyí yàopǐn
Check the Medication of the Gas Detector

 复习 Revision

连线。Match.

掐住		squeeze sth. flat
吸气球		hand
捏扁	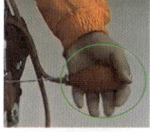	pinch
胶管		bulge
手	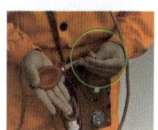	rubber hose
胀起		suction balloon

职通中文 煤矿开采技术（初级篇）

 热身 Warm-up

下列图片你认识多少？ How many of the following pictures do you know?

guījiāo
硅胶
silica gel

nàshíhuī
钠石灰
soda lime

kēlì
颗粒
particle

yánsè
颜色
color

fěnhóngsè
粉红色
pink

shēnlánsè
深蓝色
dark blue

báisè
白色
white

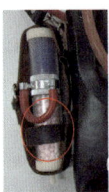
èryǎnghuàtàn xīshōuguǎn
二氧化碳 吸收管
carbon dioxide absorption tube

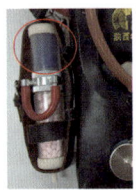
shuǐfèn xīshōuguǎn
水分 吸收管
moisture absorption tube

 学习生词 Words and Expressions  14-01

1	药品	yàopǐn	n.	medication
2	水分	shuǐfèn	n.	moisture
3	吸收管	xīshōuguǎn	n.	absorption tube

第14课 | 检查瓦检仪药品

4	内	nèi	n.	inside
5	硅胶	guījiāo	n.	silica gel
6	颗粒	kēlì	n.	particle
7	颜色	yánsè	n.	color
8	若……则……	ruò……zé……		if...then...
9	深蓝色	shēnlánsè	n.	dark blue
10	合格	hégé	adj.	qualified
11	粉红色	fěnhóngsè	n.	pink
12	需要	xūyào	v.	need
13	二氧化碳	èryǎnghuàtàn	n.	carbon dioxide
14	钠石灰	nàshíhuī	n.	soda lime
15	白色	báisè	n.	white

词语练习 Word Exercises

1. 连线。Match.

粉红色　　　　　　　　　　dark blue

白色　　　　　　　　　　　soda lime

深蓝色　　　　　　　　　　pink

二氧化碳　　　　　　　　　moisture absorption

水分吸收　　　　　　　　　carbon dioxide

硅胶　　　　　　　　　　　white

钠石灰　　　　　　　　　　silica gel

2. 看图片，将相应的字母填在括号里。Look at the pictures and fill in the corresponding letters in the brackets.

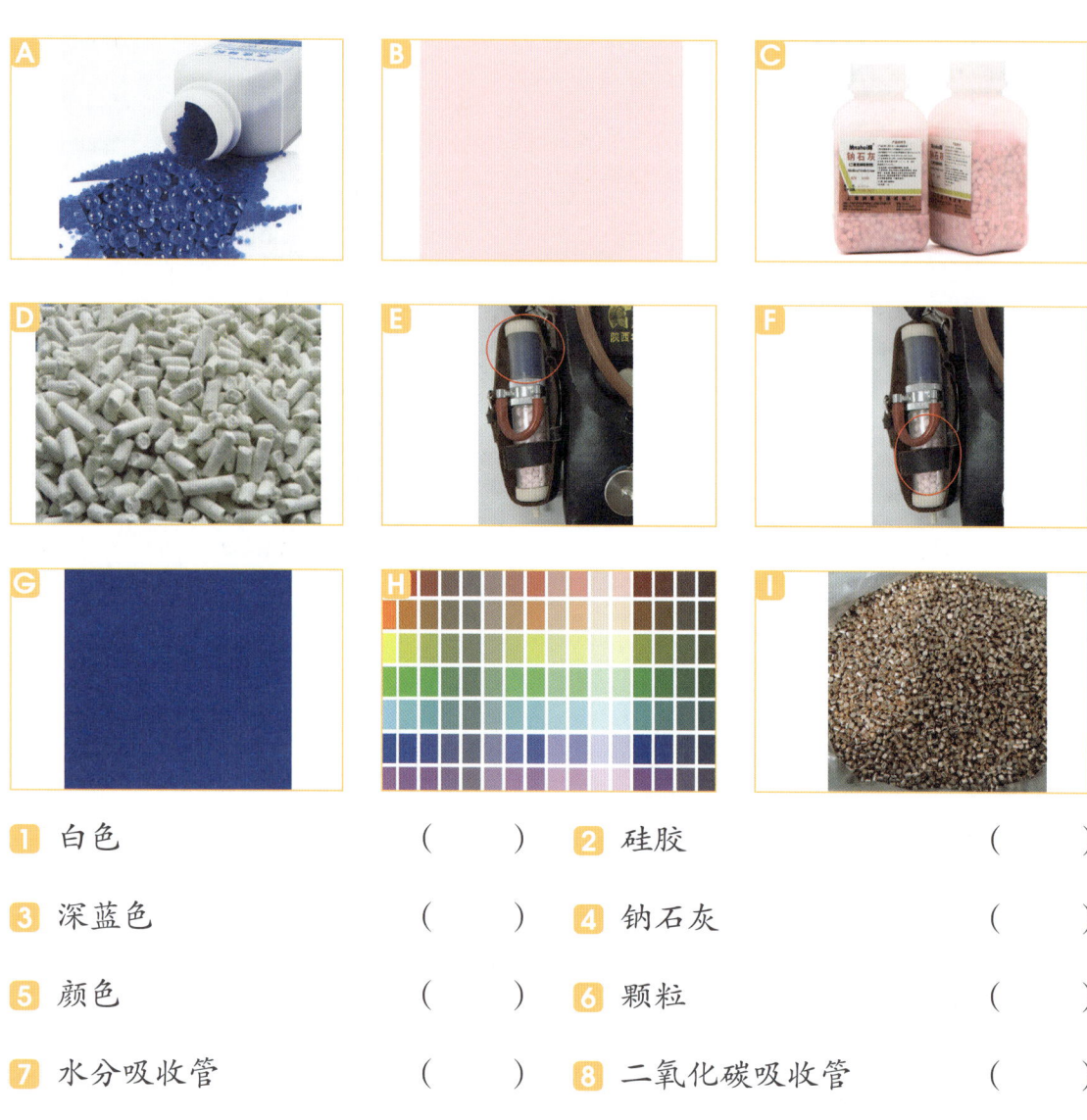

1 白色　　　　　（　）　　2 硅胶　　　　　　　（　）

3 深蓝色　　　　（　）　　4 钠石灰　　　　　　（　）

5 颜色　　　　　（　）　　6 颗粒　　　　　　　（　）

7 水分吸收管　　（　）　　8 二氧化碳吸收管　　（　）

9 粉色　　　　　（　）

第14课 | 检查瓦检仪药品

 学习课文 Text 🎧 14-02

检查瓦检仪药品
Jiǎnchá wǎjiǎnyí yàopǐn

1. 检查水分吸收管内硅胶颗粒的颜色，若是深蓝色，则合格；若是粉红色，则需要更换。

2. 检查二氧化碳吸收管内的钠石灰，若是粉红色颗粒，则合格；若是白色的，则需要更换。

Check the Medication of the Gas Detector

1. Check the color of the silica gel particles in the moisture absorption tube. If it is dark blue, it is qualified. If it is pink, it needs to be replaced.

2. Check the soda lime in the carbon dioxide absorption tube. If it is pink, it is qualified. If it is white, it needs to be replaced.

课文练习 Text Exercises

1. 根据课文内容，判断对错。Tell True (T) or False (F) according to the text.

①	水分吸收管内是硅胶颗粒。	A. 是	B. 不是
②	二氧化碳吸收管内应该是白色的钠石灰。	A. 是	B. 不是

③ 若硅胶颗粒颜色为深蓝色，则表明合格。	A. 是	B. 不是
④ 若钠石灰颗粒颜色为白色，则表明合格。	A. 是	B. 不是

2. 根据课文内容，选词填空。Choose the words to fill in the blanks according to the text.

① 水分吸收管内的药品是（　　　）。

A. 粉红色硅胶颗粒　　　B. 深蓝色硅胶颗粒　　　C. 粉红色钠石灰

② 二氧化碳吸收管内的药品是（　　　）。

A. 深蓝色硅胶颗粒　　　B. 白色钠石灰　　　C. 粉红色钠石灰

③ 检查水分吸收管内硅胶颗粒的颜色，若是（　　　），则需要更换。

A. 深蓝色　　　B. 粉红色　　　C. 白色

④ 检查二氧化碳吸收管内硅胶颗粒的颜色，若是（　　　），则需要更换。

A. 深蓝色　　　B. 粉红色　　　C. 白色

学习语法 Grammar

 语法点1 Grammar Point 1

方位词：内　The word of locality: 内

用在名词后，表示物体内部。口语中常用"里"。

It is used after a noun to indicate the interior of an object. "里" is often used in spoken Chinese.

① 检查 水分 吸收管 内 硅胶 颗粒的 颜色。Check the color of the silica gel particles in the moisture absorption tube.
Jiǎnchá shuǐfèn xīshōuguǎn nèi guījiāo kēlì de yánsè.

> Èryǎnghuàtàn xīshōuguǎn nèi de nàshíhuī bù kěyǐ shì báisè de.
>
> ② 二氧化碳 吸收管 内的钠石灰不可以是白色的。The soda lime in the carbon dioxide absorption tube cannot be white.
>
> Yào zhùyì hàngdào nèi de xìnhàodēng、chēliàng hé lùbiāo.
>
> ③ 要注意巷道 内的信号灯、车辆和路标。Pay attention to the signal lamps, vehicles, and road signs in the tunnel.

语法点1练习 Grammar Point Exercises 1

选词填空。Choose the words to fill in the blanks.

A. 内　B. 上

① 把矿灯系在皮带_____。

② 把设备放到仓库（cāngkù, warehouse）_____。

③ 在巷道_____行走要注意安全。

④ 脖子_____系一条毛巾。

语法点2 Grammar Point 2

> 若……，则……
>
> 表示假设条件关系，为书面语，口语中一般用"如果……，(就)……"。
> It indicates a hypothetical conditional relationship and is used in written Chinese. In spoken Chinese, "如果……,(就)……" is often used.
>
> Ruò guījiāo kēlì shì shēnlánsè de, zé biǎomíng hégé.
>
> ① 若硅胶颗粒是深蓝色的，则表明合格。If the silica gel particles are dark blue, it indicates that they are qualified.
>
> Ruò guījiāo kēlì shì fěnhóngsè de, zé xūyào gēnghuàn.
>
> ② 若硅胶颗粒是粉红色的，则需要更换。If the silica gel particles are pink, they need to be replaced.

3. Ruò guà yǒu "jìnzhǐ rù nèi" de biāozhì, zé bù kěyǐ jìnrù.
若挂有"禁止入内"的标志，则不可以进入。If there is a sign that reads "No Entry", entry is not allowed.

语法点 2 练习 Grammar Point Exercises 2

用"若……，则……"改写句子。Rewrite the sentences with "若……，则……".

1. 硅胶颗粒是深蓝色的，表明合格。

2. 钠石灰颗粒是白色的，需要更换。

3. 乘坐罐笼下井，要听指挥、站稳扶好。

4. 如果矿灯有问题，需要更换矿灯。

汉字书写 Writing Chinese Characters

mù
木　木　木　木　木

huī
灰　灰　灰　灰　灰　灰　灰

shù
束　束　束　束　束　束　束

huī
恢　恢　恢　恢　恢　恢　恢　恢

第 14 课 | 检查瓦检仪药品

职业拓展 Career Insight

Composition of Optical Gas Detector

The optical gas detector mainly consists of three systems: air path, light path, and circuit. Specifically, it includes an eyepiece, a micro-reading window, a main adjustment screw, a light source switch button, a fine adjustment screw, a micro-reading switch, a moisture absorption tube, a carbon dioxide absorption tube, and an air chamber.

词语 Words

朗读下面的短语。Read aloud the following phrases.

1. 检查药品　　　检查颜色　　　更换药品
2. 吸收水分　　　吸收二氧化碳　　需要更换
3. 颜色合格　　　药品合格　　　硅胶颗粒

语法 Grammar

朗读下面的句子。Read aloud the following sentences.

1. 检查水分吸收管内硅胶颗粒的颜色。
2. 检查二氧化碳吸收管内钠石灰的颜色。
3. 若硅胶颗粒是深蓝色的，则表明合格。
4. 若硅胶颗粒是粉红色的，则需要更换。

课文理解 Text Comprehension

复述课文内容。Retell the text.

检查瓦检仪药品时，先检查水分吸收管内的 _____ 的颜色，若是 _____，则 _____；若是 _____，则 _____。然后检查二氧化碳吸收管内的 _____，若是粉红色颗粒，则 _____；若是白色的，则需要 _____。

第 15 课 Lesson 15

Jiǎnchá wǎsī qìtǐ nóngdù
检查瓦斯气体浓度
Check the Gas Concentration

 复习 Revision

连线。Match.

钠石灰		white
深蓝色		dark blue
二氧化碳吸收管		silica gel
硅胶		moisture absorption tube
白色		soda lime
水分吸收管		carbon dioxide absorption tube

131

职通中文 煤矿开采技术（初级篇）

热身 Warm-up

下列图片你认识多少？ How many of the following pictures do you know?

wǎsī
瓦斯
gas

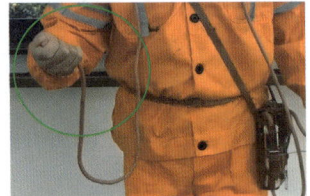
jìnqì jiāoguǎnkǒu
进气胶管口
air inlet rubber nozzle

bēidài
背带
shoulder strap

guà
挂
hang

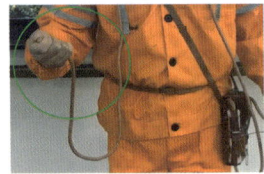
wòzhù
握住
hold

wēidúshù shìchuāng
微读数 视窗
micro-reading window

学习生词 Words and Expressions 15-01

1	瓦斯	wǎsī	n.	gas
2	气体	qìtǐ	n.	gas
3	浓度	nóngdù	n.	concentration
4	背带	bēidài	n.	shoulder strap
5	握	wò	v.	hold
6	进气	jìnqì	v.	intake (air)
7	胶管口	jiāoguǎnkǒu	n.	rubber nozzle

8	伸入	shēnrù	phr.	insert into
9	检测区	jiǎncèqū	n.	detection zone
10	次	cì	m.	time
11	吸入	xīrù	phr.	inhale
12	微读数视窗	wēidúshù shìchuāng	phr.	micro-reading window
13	读出	dúchū	phr.	read
14	数据	shùjù	n.	data

词语练习 Word Exercises

1. 看图片，将相应的字母填在括号里。Look at the pictures and fill in the corresponding letters in the brackets.

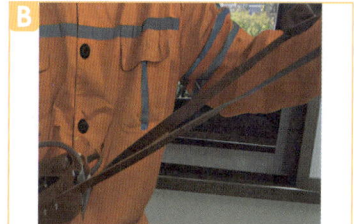
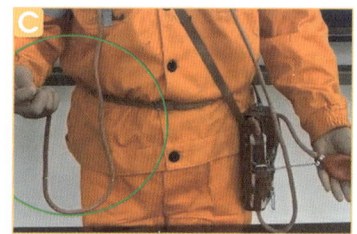
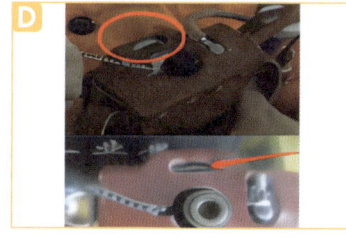

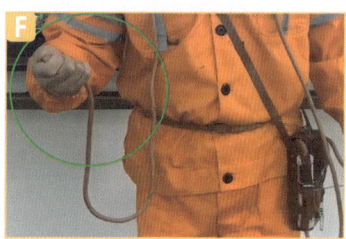

❶ 微读数视窗（　） ❷ 挂在脖子上（　） ❸ 瓦斯（　）
❹ 进气胶管口（　） ❺ 背带（　） ❻ 握住（　）

2. 朗读词语搭配。Read the word collocations.

❶ 吸入	吸入瓦斯气体	❷ 伸入	伸入巷道
	吸入二氧化碳气体		伸入工作面
❸ 握住	握住进气胶管口	❹ 读出	读出数字
	握住瓦检仪		读出汉字

 学习课文 Text 🎧 15-02

Jiǎnchá wǎsī qìtǐ nóngdù
检查瓦斯气体浓度

Bǎ wǎjiǎnyí de bēidài guà zài bózi shang.
1. 把瓦检仪的背带挂在脖子上。

Yì zhī shǒu wòzhù jìnqì jiāoguǎnkǒu, shēnrù jiǎncèqū.
2. 一只手握住进气胶管口，伸入检测区。

Lìng yì zhī shǒu niē xīqìqiú 5~6 cì, xīrù wǎsī qìtǐ.
3. 另一只手捏吸气球5～6次，吸入瓦斯气体。

Ànxia ànniǔ, guānchá mùjìng hé wēidúshù shìchuāng, dúchū shùjù.
4. 按下按钮，观察目镜和微读数视窗，读出数据。

Check the Gas Concentration

1. Hang the shoulder strap of the gas detector on the neck.

第 15 课 | 检查瓦斯气体浓度

2. Hold the air inlet rubber nozzle with one hand and insert it into the detection zone.

3. Squeeze the suction balloon with the other hand 5-6 times to inhale gas.

4. Press the button, observe the eyepiece and micro-reading window, and read the data.

课文练习 Text Exercises

1. 根据课文内容，判断对错。Tell True (T) or False (F) according to the text.

Statements	Answer
❶ 在检测瓦斯气体时，先要把瓦检仪的背带挂在脖子上。	A. 是　　B. 不是
❷ 一只手握住进气胶管口，伸入检测区，不需要捏吸气球。	A. 是　　B. 不是
❸ 吸入瓦斯气体后，按下按钮，只需观察目镜，读出数据。	A. 是　　B. 不是
❹ 吸入瓦斯气体后，按下按钮，只需观察微读数视窗，读出数据。	A. 是　　B. 不是

2. 根据课文内容，选词填空。Choose the words to fill in the blanks according to the text.

❶ 检测瓦斯气体浓度时，一只手握住（　　），深入检测区。

　A. 按钮　　　　　B. 吸气球　　　　　C. 进气胶管口

❷ 另一只手捏吸气球（　　）次，吸入瓦斯气体。

　A. 2～3　　　　　B. 5～6　　　　　C. 8～9

135

3 吸入瓦斯气体后，按下按钮，观察目镜和（　　），读出数据。

　　A. 胶管　　　　　B. 微读数视窗　　　　C. 吸气球

4 一只手握住进气胶管口，伸入（　　）。

　　A. 巷道　　　　　B. 工作面　　　　C. 检测区

 学习语法 Grammar

 语法点1 Grammar Point 1

动量词：次　The measure word for verbs: 次

在动词后表示动作的数量。用于反复出现或可能反复出现的事情。常用结构为"动词 + 数词 + 次（+ 宾语）"。

It is used after a verb to indicate how many times that an action has been performed. It is used for events that have happened repeatedly or events that are likely to happen repeatedly. The common structure is "verb + numeral + 次 (+ object)".

　　　　　Niē xīqìqiú　5~6 cì.
1 捏吸气球5～6次。Squeeze the suction ballon 5-6 times.

　　　　Tā jīntiān yào xià sān cì jǐng.
2 他今天要下三次井。He will go down the shaft three times today.

　　　Nǐ zài jiǎnchá yí cì.
3 你再检查一次。Check it again.

 语法点1练习 Grammar Point Exercises 1

连词成句。Rearrange the words to form sentences.

1 ①参加　②他　③必须　④两次　⑤安全培训

第15课 | 检查瓦斯气体浓度

2 ①今天　②乘坐　③三次　④需要　⑤猴车

___

3 ①我　②下　③准备　④一次　⑤井

___

4 ①可以　②你　③吸气球　④捏　⑤五次

___

语法点 2　Grammar Point 2

趋向补语：出（来）　The complement of direction: 出（来）

"出（来）"在动词后，表示动作由内而外的方向。

"出（来）" is used after a verb to indicate the direction of an action from inside out.

1　Guānchá mùjìng hé wēidúshù shìchuāng, dúchū shùjù.
　观察目镜和微读数视窗，读出数据。Observe the eyepiece and micro-reading window to read the data.

2　Qǐng xiěchū nǐ de míngzi.
　请写出你的名字。Please write down your name.

3　Gōngrén ná chulai yí gè kuàngdēng.
　工人拿出来一个矿灯。The worker took out a mining lamp.

语法点 2 练习　Grammar Point Exercises 2

连词成句。Rearrange the words to form sentences.

1 ①大声　②说　③你　④的　⑤出　⑥名字

___

2 ①工人　②拿　③一个　④出来　⑤自救器

___

3 ①请 ②观察 ③读 ④出 ⑤数据

4 ①使用 ②自救器 ③写 ④出 ⑤的 ⑥步骤

汉字书写 Writing Chinese Characters

职业拓展 Career Insight

Bird's Nest

Bird's Nest (The National Stadium) is in the south of the central area of Beijing Olympic Park. It was the main stadium for the 2008 Beijing Olympics, covering an area of 204,000 m^2 and a floor area of 258,000 m^2 to accommodate 91,000 spectators. It witnessed the opening and closing ceremonies of the

Olympic and Paralympic Games, as well as the finals of athletics and football competitions. After the Olympics, it has become a large professional venue for Beijing citizens to participate in and enjoy sports activities and sports entertainment, and has become a landmark sports building and Olympic heritage.

小结 Summary

词语 Words

朗读下面的短语。Read aloud the following phrases.

1. 伸入检测区
2. 握住胶管口
3. 按下按钮
4. 观察目镜
5. 吸入气体
6. 捏住气球
7. 读出数据
8. 观察视窗

语法 Grammar

朗读下面的句子。Read aloud the following sentences.

1. 捏吸气球5～6次。
2. 你再检查一次。
3. 观察微读数视窗，读出数据。
4. 请写出你的名字。

课文理解 Text Comprehension

复述课文内容。Retell the text.

　　检查瓦斯气体浓度时，要把瓦检仪的背带挂在_____上。一只手握住进气_____，伸入_____。另一只手捏_____5～6次，吸入_____气体。按下按钮，观察_____和微读数视窗，读出_____。

第 16 课 Lesson 16

Cè fēng qián de zhǔnbèi
测风前的准备
Preparation Before Wind Measurement

复习 Revision

连线。Match.

背带		gas
挂在		hang sth. on ...
瓦斯		micro-reading window
进气胶管口		hold
微读数视窗		shoulder strap
握住	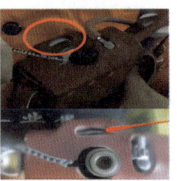	air inlet rubber nozzle

第 16 课 | 测风前的准备

 **热身 Warm-up**

下列图片你认识多少？ How many of the following pictures do you know?

fēngbiǎo
风表
anemometer

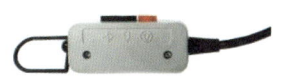

kāiguān
开关
switch

jìlùběn
记录本
logbook

zhǐzhēn
指针
pointer

miǎobiǎo
秒表
stopwatch

 **学习生词 Words and Expressions** 🎧 16-01

1	测风	cè fēng	phr.	anemometry
2	风表	fēngbiǎo	n.	anemometer
3	指针	zhǐzhēn	n.	pointer
4	等	děng	part.	etc.
5	部件	bùjiàn	n.	component
6	灵活	línghuó	adj.	flexible
7	可靠	kěkào	adj.	reliable
8	秒表	miǎobiǎo	n.	stopwatch

141

9	记录本	jìlùběn	n.	logbook
10	皮尺	píchǐ	n.	tape measure
11	仪器	yíqì	n.	instrument
12	各个	gègè	pron.	every
13	能	néng	opt.	can

词语练习 Word Exercises

1. 看图片，将相应的字母填在括号里。**Look at the pictures and fill in the corresponding letters in the brackets.**

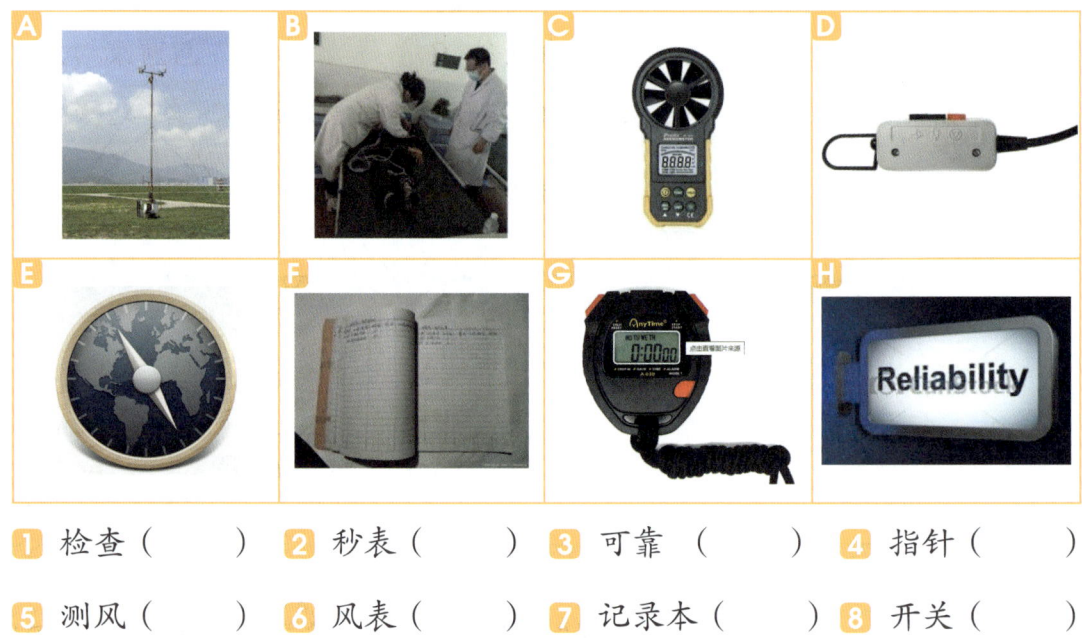

1 检查（　　） 2 秒表（　　） 3 可靠（　　） 4 指针（　　）

5 测风（　　） 6 风表（　　） 7 记录本（　　） 8 开关（　　）

2. 朗读词语搭配。**Read the word collocations.**

❶ 灵活	灵活可靠	flexible and reliable
	灵活应用	flexible application

❷	破损	外壳有破损	There are some damages to the shell.
		皮尺有破损	There are some damages to the tape measure.
❸	校正	校正仪表	instrument calibration
		地形校正	topographic correction
❹	准备好	准备好风表	prepare the anemometer
		准备好记录本	prepare the logbook

学习课文 Text 🎧 16-02

测风前的准备
Cè fēng qián de zhǔnbèi

测风前要检查风表的开关、指针等部件是否灵活可靠,要检查风表的外壳有没有破损。准备好秒表、记录本、皮尺、瓦检仪等相关仪器,各个仪器检查合格后,才能下井测风。

Preparation Before wind measurement

Before wind measurement, check whether the switch, pointer, and other components of the anemometer are flexible and reliable, and whether there are any damages to the shell of the anemometer. Prepare relevant instruments such as the stopwatch, the logbook, the tape measure, the gas detector, etc. Only after checking all the instruments can the downhole wind measurement be started.

课文练习 Text Exercises

1. 根据课文内容，判断对错。Tell True (T) or False (F) according to the text.

Statements	Answer
① 风表开关、指针必须灵活可靠。	A. 是　　B. 不是
② 风表外壳可以有破损。	A. 是　　B. 不是
③ 下井前必须检查所有仪器。	A. 是　　B. 不是
④ 测风前要准备好风表、秒表、皮尺、记录本等。	A. 是　　B. 不是

2. 根据课文内容，选词填空。Choose the words to fill in the blanks according to the text.

① 风表（　　）、指针灵活可靠。

A. 元件　　　　B. 开关　　　　C. 外观

② 检查风表的（　　）有无破损。

A. 外观　　　　B. 状态　　　　C. 外壳

③ 秒表的开关和指针必须（　　）。

A. 灵活　　　　B. 松动　　　　C. 固定

④ 所有的仪器检查（　　）后，才能下井。

A. 灵活　　　　B. 合格　　　　C. 外壳

第 16 课 ｜ 测风前的准备

学习语法 Grammar

语法点 1 Grammar Point 1

助词：等 The particle: 等
表示列举未尽，可以叠用为"等等"。
It indicates incomplete enumeration and can be used repeatedly as "等等".

1. Fēngbiǎo de kāiguān、zhǐzhēn děng bùjiàn yào línghuó kěkào.
   风表的开关、指针等部件要灵活可靠。The switch, pointer, etc. of the anemometer should be flexible and reliable.

2. Cèfēng yào zhǔnbèi hǎo miǎobiǎo、píchǐ、wǎjiǎnyí děng yíqì.
   测风要准备好秒表、皮尺、瓦检仪等仪器。The stopwatch, the tape measure, the gas detector, etc. should be prepared before wind measurement.

3. Hàngdào de xíngzhuàng yǒu tīxíng、yuánxíng、gǒngxíng děng.
   巷道的形状有梯形、圆形、拱形等。The shapes of the tunnels include trapezoids, circles, arches, etc.

语法点 1 练习 Grammar Point Exercises 1

用"等"完成句子。Complete the sentences with "等".

1. 安全培训内容有_____。
2. 巷道的形状有_____。
3. 井下行走时，要注意_____。
4. 煤矿是由_____组成的。

语法点 2 Grammar Point 2

能愿动词：能 The optative verb: 能
表示有条件做或情理上许可。
It indicates conditional or reasonable permission.

145

> Gègè yíqì jiǎnchá hégé hòu, cái néng xià jǐng cè fēng.
> ① 各个仪器检查合格后，才能 下 井 测 风。Only after checking all the instruments can the downhole wind measurement be started.
>
> Xuánzhuǎn mùjìng néng tiáozhěng fēnhuábǎn qīngxīdù.
> ② 旋转 目镜 能 调整 分划板清晰度。Rotating the eyepiece can adjust the clearness degree of the reticle.
>
> Nǐngsōng dēngpào hòugài néng tiáozhěng gānshè tiáowén qīngxīdù.
> ③ 拧松 灯泡 后盖能 调整 干涉 条纹 清晰度。Unscrewing the rear cover of the bulb can adjust the clearness degree of the interference fringes.

语法点 2 练习 Grammar Point Exercises 2

用"能"或"不能"填空。Fill in the blanks with "能" or "不能".

① 做好准备工作后才_____下井。　　　　A. 能　　B. 不能

② _____进入挂有"禁止入内"警告标志的巷道。　A. 能　　B. 不能

③ 罐笼运行时，_____玩耍、打闹。　　　A. 能　　B. 不能

④ 乘坐猴车时，_____离开座位。　　　　A. 能　　B. 不能

 汉字书写 Writing Chinese Characters

dāo 刀 刀
刀 刀 刀 刀 刀

rèn 刃 刃 刃
刃 刃 刃 刃 刃

yán 炎 炎 炎 炎 炎 炎 炎 炎
炎 炎 炎 炎 炎

第 16 课 | 测风前的准备

dàn
淡 淡 淡 淡 淡 淡 淡 淡 淡 淡 淡 淡
淡 淡 淡 淡 淡

职业拓展 Career Insight

Ventilation Resistance Tester

The ventilation resistance tester adopts the "barometer base point measurement method" to measure the ventilation resistance and related ventilation parameters of mine tunnels, helping workers understand the resistance distribution in the mine ventilation system. In addition, it provides a basis for the formulation and implementation of safety technical measures in the mine, and offers reliable basic data for mine ventilation design, network solution, ventilation system transformation, fire control, etc.

小结 Summary

 词语 Words

根据课文内容，选择恰当的词语。Choose the appropriate words according to the text.

_____前要检查_____的开关、_____等部件是否_____可靠，要检查风表的外壳有没有破损。

　　A. 灵活　　　B. 指针　　　C. 测风　　　D. 风表

语法 Grammar

朗读下面的句子。Read aloud the following sentences.

1. 风表的开关、指针等部件要灵活可靠。

2. 测风要准备好秒表、皮尺、瓦检仪等仪器。

3. 各个仪器检查合格后,才能下井测风。

4. 旋转目镜能调整分划板清晰度。

课文理解 Text Comprehension

根据课文内容,判断对错。Tell True (T) or False (F) according to the text.

测风前要检查风表。 Check the anemometer before the wind measurement.	A. 是　　B. 不是
测风前检查风表开关、指针等。 Check the switch, pointer, etc. of the anemometer before the wind measurement.	A. 是　　B. 不是
测风时不需要秒表、记录本等。 The stopwatch, the logbook, etc. are not necessary during the anemometry work.	A. 是　　B. 不是
各仪器检查合格后,才能下井测风。 Only after checking all the instruments can the downhole wind measurement be started.	A. 是　　B. 不是

第 17 课 lesson 17

Cè fēng de fāngfǎ
测风的方法
Anemometry Method

复习 Revision

连线。**Match.**

指针		switch
记录本		anemometer
秒表		pointer
风表		logbook
开关		stopwatch

149

职通中文 煤矿开采技术（初级篇）

 **热身 Warm-up**

下列图片你认识多少？ How many of the following pictures do you know?

fēngbiǎo
风表
anemometer

miǎobiǎo
秒表
stopwatch

chuízhí
垂直
vertical

zhǐzhēn
指针
pointer

dúshù
读数
reading

fēnzhōng
分钟
minute

 **学习生词 Words and Expressions**  17-01

1	方法	fāngfǎ	n.	method
2	回零	huílíng	v.	return to zero
3	让	ràng	v.	let
4	保持	bǎochí	v.	keep, maintain
5	垂直	chuízhí	v.	vertical

第 17 课 | 测风的方法

6	风流	fēngliú	n.	wind flow
7	方向	fāngxiàng	n.	direction
8	空转	kōngzhuàn	v.	idle (of a motor, etc.)
9	秒	miǎo	m.	second
10	分钟	fēnzhōng	m.	minute
11	关闭	guānbì	v.	turn off
12	读数	dúshù	n.	reading

词语练习 Word Exercises

1. 看图片，将相应的字母填在括号里。Look at the pictures and fill in the corresponding letters in the brackets.

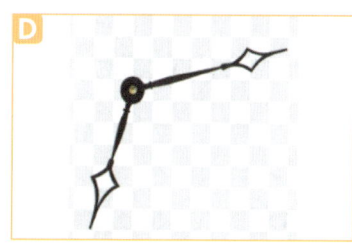

❶ 秒表　　　（　） ❷ 分钟　　　（　） ❸ 垂直　　　（　）

❹ 读数　　　（　） ❺ 指针　　　（　） ❻ 风表　　　（　）

2. 根据课文内容，选词填空。Choose the words to fill in the blanks according to the text.

① 取出（　）测量风速。 A. 风表　B. 指针　C. 分钟

② 让秒表的（　）回零。  A. 指针　B. 风表　C. 风流

③ 让风表和风流方向（　）。  A. 连接　B. 平行　C. 垂直

④ 读出风表的（　）。  A. 读数　B. 秒　C. 秒

学习课文　Text　🎧 17-02

Cè fēng de fāngfǎ
测风的方法

Xiān ànxia fēngbiǎo hé miǎobiǎo de huílíng ànniǔ, ràng zhǐzhēn
先按下风表和秒表的回零按钮，让指针
huílíng. Ránhòu shǒu wò fēngbiǎo, bǎochí fēngbiǎo chuízhí yú fēngliú
回零。然后手握风表，保持风表垂直于风流
de fāngxiàng, ràng fēngbiǎo kōngzhuàn 30 miǎo hòu, tóngshí dǎkāi fēngbiǎo
的方向，让风表空转30秒后，同时打开风表
hé miǎobiǎo kāiguān. Yì fēnzhōng hòu tóngshí guānbì fēngbiǎo、miǎobiǎo
和秒表开关。一分钟后同时关闭风表、秒表
kāiguān, dúchū fēngbiǎo de dúshù.
开关，读出风表的读数。

第 17 课 | 测风的方法

Anemometry Method

Press the zeroing buttons of the anemometer and of the stopwatch to let the pointer zero. Then hold the anemometer and keep it vertical to the direction of the wind flow. Let the anemometer idle for 30 seconds and then turn on the switches of the anemometer and of the stopwatch simultaneously. Turn off the switches of the anemometer and of the stopwatch simultaneously in a minute and read out the data on the anemometer.

课文练习 Text Exercises

1. 根据课文内容，判断对错。Tell True (T) or False (F) according to the text.

Statements	Answer	
① 在开始测风前，先要让风表和秒表的指针回零。	A. 是	B. 不是
② 在测风时，风表和风流方向垂直。	A. 是	B. 不是
③ 在测风前，风表需要空转 30 分钟。	A. 是	B. 不是
④ 风表空转后，要同时打开风表和秒表开关。	A. 是	B. 不是

2. 根据课文内容，选词填空。Choose the words to fill in the blanks according to the text.

① 测量风速时使用风表和_____。　　A. 秒表　　B. 分钟

② 测风时要保持风表与风流风向_____。　　A. 连接　　B. 垂直

③ 测风前，风表需空转_____。　　A.30 秒　　B.30 分钟

④ 风表空转后，需要_____。
　　A. 同时按下风表和秒表开关　　B. 先按下风表开关，然后按下秒表开关

学习语法 Grammar

语法点 1 Grammar Point 1

> **用"让"的兼语句** Pivotal sentences with "让"
> 表示使得产生一定的结果。常用结构为"让 + 名词 + 动词性词语"。
> It indicates producing a certain result. The common structure is "让 + noun + verbal word".

1. Ràng fēngbiǎo de zhǐzhēn huílíng.
   让 风表 的 指针 回零。Let the pointer of the anemometer zero.
2. Ràng gōngrén xuéxí ānquán zhīshi.
   让 工人 学习 安全 知识。Let employees learn safety knowledge.
3. Ràng tóngxuémen liànxí Hànzì.
   让 同学们 练习 汉字。Let students practice Chinese characters.

语法点 1 练习 Grammar Point Exercises 1

连词成句。Rearrange the words to form sentences.

1. ①让 ②回零 ③风表 ④指针 ⑤的

2. ①风表 ②保持 ③让 ④的 ⑤垂直 ⑥方向 ⑦风流

3. ①工人 ②让 ③读数 ④表 ⑤读出 ⑥的

4. ①所有 ②进入 ③让 ④人员 ⑤风门

第 17 课 | 测风的方法

语法点 1　Grammar Point 1

时间单位词：秒、分钟、小时　Measure words for time: 秒，分钟，小时

"秒、分钟、小时"都是时间单位词。其中"秒、分钟"可以直接与数词搭配，"小时"可直接与数词搭配，前边也可用量词"个"。

"秒"，"分钟"，and "小时" are measure words for time. "秒" and "分钟" can be directly paired with numerals. "小时" can be directly paired with a numeral, and it can also be preceded by the measure word "个".

---

1. Ràng fēngbiǎo kōngzhuàn 30 miǎo.
   让　风表　空转　30 秒。Let the anemometer idle for 30 seconds.

2. Yì fēnzhōng hòu guānbì fēngbiǎo kāiguān.
   一分钟　后关闭　风表　开关。Turn off the switch of the anemometer in one minute.

3. Wǒmen jīntiān gōngzuò 8 gè xiǎoshí.
   我们今天工作 8 个 小时。We work for 8 hours today.

语法点 2 练习　Grammar Point Exercises 2

选词填空。Choose the words to fill in the blanks.

A. 秒　B. 分钟　C. 小时

1. 今天我们上 50 ＿＿＿＿ 中文课。

2. 风表要先空转 30 ＿＿＿＿ 。

3. 让工人们休息 10 ＿＿＿＿ 。

4. 罐笼从上向下运行 2 ＿＿＿＿ 。

汉字书写 Writing Chinese Characters

文化拓展 Culture Insight

Qin Opera

Qin opera is a folk art form of Han ethnic group. It was originated in ancient Shaanxi and Gansu and evolved in Chang'an — the political, economic and cultural center of ancient China. It was formed from the creation of generations of people and was named as the "Qin opera" as the Guanzhong area has been called "Qin" since Zhou Dynasty. It is also known as "Bangzi Tune" because it uses jujube wood stick as a percussion instrument. Further more, it is commonly known as "Guangguangzi" since it produces a "Guangguang" sound.

第17课 | 测风的方法

小结 Summary

词语 Words

根据课文内容，选择恰当的词语。Choose the appropriate words according to the text.

先按下风表和 _____ 的回零按钮，让指针 _____。然后手握风表，保持风表 _____ 于风流的方向，让风表空转 _____ 秒后，_____ 打开风表和秒表 _____。一分钟后同时关闭风表、秒表开关，读出风表的读数。

A. 秒表　　B. 30　　C. 回零　　D. 同时　　E. 开关　　F. 垂直

语法 Grammar

朗读下面的句子。Read aloud the following sentences.

1. 让风表的指针回零。
2. 一分钟后关闭风表开关。
3. 让风表空转30秒。
4. 我们今天工作8个小时。

课文理解 Text Comprehension

根据课文内容，判断对错。Tell True (T) or False (F) according to the text.

1 测风时，风表要和风流方向垂直。	A. 是　　B. 不是
2 测风前，风表需要空转30分钟。	A. 是　　B. 不是
3 风表空转后，要同时打开风表和秒表开关。	A. 是　　B. 不是
4 测风时，不需要按下风表的回零按钮。	A. 是　　B. 不是

第18课 Lesson18

Jiǎnchá méidiànzuàn
检查煤电钻
Check the Electric Coal Drill

复习 Revision

连线。Match.

秒表	垂直	指针	分钟	读数	风表
vertical	reading	anemometer	pointer	minute	stopwatch

热身 Warm-up

下列图片你认识多少？How many of the following pictures do you know?

méibì
煤壁
coal wall

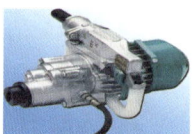

méidiànzuàn
煤电钻
electric coal drill

luósī
螺丝
screw

méidiànzuàn kāiguān
煤电钻 开关
electric coal drill switch

méi
煤
coal

méikuàng dǐngbǎn
煤矿 顶板
coal mine roof

 第 18 课 | 检查煤电钻

学习生词 Words and Expressions  18-01

1	煤电钻	méidiànzuàn	n.	electric coal drill
2	首先	shǒuxiān	pron.	first
3	螺丝	luósī	n.	screw
4	松动	sōngdòng	v.	loosen
5	其次	qícì	pron.	secondly
6	地点	dìdiǎn	n.	place
7	顶板	dǐngbǎn	n.	roof
8	煤壁	méibì	n.	coal wall
9	情况	qíngkuàng	n.	condition, situation
10	只有	zhǐyǒu	conj.	only
11	进行	jìnxíng	v.	conduct
12	实验	shíyàn	v.	experiment
13	确保	quèbǎo	v.	ensure
14	正常	zhèngcháng	adj.	normal

词语练习 Word Exercises

1. 看图片，将相应的字母填在括号里。Look at the pictures and fill in the corresponding letters in the brackets.

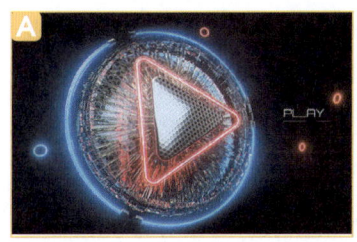 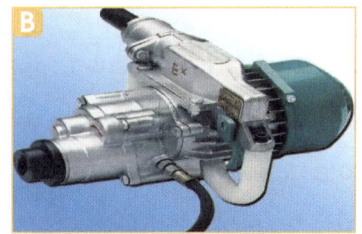 

1. 煤电钻　　（　　）　2. 按钮　　（　　）　3. 煤炭　　（　　）

4. 螺丝　　（　　）　5. 煤电钻开关（　　）　6. 煤壁　　（　　）

2. 选词填空。 Choose the words to fill in the blanks.

1. （　　）煤电钻外壳　　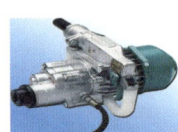　　A. 检查　B. 安装　C. 观察

2. 检查煤电钻（　　）　　　　A. 钻头　B. 外壳　C. 电线

3. 检查煤电钻螺丝有无（　　）　　A. 脱落　B. 松动　C. 损坏

4. 检查开关是否（　　）　　　A. 灵活　B. 完好　C. 安全

学习课文　Text　🎧 18-02

Jiǎnchá méidiànzuàn
检查煤电钻

Shǒuxiān, jiǎnchá méidiànzuàn wàiké yǒu wú sǔnhuài, luósī yǒu wú
首先，检查煤电钻外壳有无损坏，螺丝有无

第18课 | 检查煤电钻

松动，开关是否灵活。其次，检查工作地点的顶板、煤壁情况，只有在安全可靠的地点，才能进行工作。最后，进行空转实验，确保煤电钻运行正常。

Check the Electric Coal Drill

Firstly, check whether there is any damage to the shell of the electric coal drill, whether the screws are loose, and whether the switch is flexible. Secondly, check the condition of the roof and the coal wall at the workplace, and only work at a safe and reliable place. Finally, conduct the idling experiment to ensure the normal operation of the electric coal drill.

课文练习 Text Exercises

1. 根据课文内容，判断对错。Tell True (T) or False (F) according to the text.

Statements	Answer
❶ 应检查煤电钻外壳有无损坏。	A. 是　　B. 不是
❷ 应检查煤电钻螺丝有无松动。	A. 是　　B. 不是
❸ 应检查工作地点的顶板、煤壁情况，只有在安全可靠的地点才能进行工作。	A. 是　　B. 不是
❹ 检查煤电钻时进行空转实验，确保煤电钻运行正常。	A. 是　　B. 不是

2. 根据课文内容，选词填空。Choose the words to fill in the blanks according to the text.

1️⃣ 要检查煤电钻外壳有无损坏，螺丝有无（　　　）。

　　A. 损坏　　　　　　B. 松动　　　　　　C. 掉落

2️⃣ 要检查工作地点的顶板和煤壁是否（　　　）。

　　A. 安全可靠　　　　B. 冒顶片帮　　　　C. 滴水漏水

3️⃣ 检查煤电钻前要（　　　）。

　　A. 进行空转实验　　B. 注意瓦斯浓度　　C. 集中精神

4️⃣ 要检查煤电钻的开关（　　　）。

　　A. 有无破损　　　　B. 是否灵活　　　　C. 有无松动

学习语法 Grammar

 语法点1 Grammar Point 1

首先……，其次……，最后……

用于表达时间前后相续的三个动作行为。

It is used to indicate three consecutive actions.

1️⃣ Shǒuxiān, jiǎnchá méidiànzuàn. Qícì, jiǎnchá gōngzuò dìdiǎn. Zuìhòu, jìnxíng kōngzhuàn shíyàn.
首先，检查 煤电钻。其次，检查 工作 地点。最后，进行 空转 实验。 Firstly, check the electric coal drill; secondly, check the workplace. Finally, conduct the idling experiment.

2️⃣ Shǒuxiān, ràng fēngbiǎo zhǐzhēn huílíng. Qícì, ràng fēngbiǎo kōngzhuàn 30 miǎo. Zuìhòu, tóngshí dǎkāi fēngbiǎo hé miǎobiǎo kāiguān.
首先，让 风表 指针 回零。其次，让 风表 空转 30 秒。最后，同时打开 风表 和 秒表 开关。Firstly, let the pointer of the anemometer zero;

secondly, let the anemometer idle for 30 seconds; finally, turn on the switches of the anemometer and of the stopwatch simultaneously.

3 Shǒuxiān, jiǎnchá fēngbiǎo de bùjiàn hé wàiké. Qícì, zhǔnbèi hǎo xiāngguān yíqì. Zuìhòu, xià jǐng cè fēng.
首先，检查风表的部件和外壳。其次，准备好相关仪器。最后，下井测风。Firstly, check the components and the shell of the anemometer; secondly, prepare relevant instruments; finally, conduct the downhole wind measurement.

语法点1练习 Grammar Point Exercises 1

选择恰当的选项填空。Choose the appropriate options to fill in the blanks.

检查瓦斯气体浓度时，首先，_____，其次，_____，_____，最后，_____。

A. 一手握住进气胶管口，伸入检测区

B. 按下按钮，观察目镜和微读数视窗，读出数据

C. 另一手捏吸气球5～6次，吸入瓦斯气体

D. 把瓦检仪的背带挂在脖子上

动词：进行 The verb: 进行

表示从事（某种活动）。
It indicates engaging in (an activity).

1 Zhǐyǒu zài ānquán kěkào de dìdiǎn, cái néng jìnxíng gōngzuò.
只有在安全可靠的地点，才能进行工作。Work can only be conducted in a safe and reliable place.

2 Wǒmen míngtiān yào jìnxíng shíyàn.
我们明天要进行实验。We will conduct an experiment tomorrow.

3 Shíyàn yíqì jīntiān xiàwǔ jìnxíng jiǎnxiū.
实验仪器今天下午进行检修。The experimental instruments will be maintained this afternoon.

语法点 2 练习 Grammar Point Exercises 2

连词成句。Rearrange the words to form sentences.

1. ①下午 ②我们 ③今天 ④要进行 ⑤实验

2. ①做好 ②工作 ③进行 ④才能 ⑤准备

3. ①仪器 ②实验 ③检修 ④要 ⑤进行

4. ①浓度 ②进行 ③要 ④气体 ⑤检查

汉字书写 Writing Chinese Characters

第18课 | 检查煤电钻

职业拓展 Career Insight

Requirements for the Downhole Work

Before the downhole work, prepare the miner's lamp and the self-rescuer, and then check the self-rescuer. During the downhole work, do not strike the lamp box or the lamp cap, do not open the lamp cap or the battery box cover to avoid accidents caused by electric sparks.

小结 Summary

本课词语 Words

朗读下面的短语。Read aloud the following phrases.

| 外壳损坏 | 螺丝松动 | 开关灵活 | 地点可靠 |
| 工作地点 | 运行正常 | 检查合格 | 空转实验 |

语法 Grammar

朗读下面的句子。 Read aloud the following sentences.

1. 首先，检查煤电钻。其次，检查工作地点。最后，进行空转实验。

2. 首先，让风表指针回零。其次，让风表空转 30 秒。最后，同时打开风表和秒表开关。

3. 只有在安全可靠的地点，才能进行工作。

4. 我们明天要进行实验。

课文理解 Text Comprehension

复述课文内容。 Retell the text.

检查煤电钻时,首先,要检查煤电钻_____有无损坏,螺丝有无_____,开关是否_____。其次,检查工作地点的_____、_____情况,只有在安全可靠的地点,才能_____工作。最后,进行空转_____,确保煤电钻运行_____。

第 19 课 Lesson 19

操作煤电钻
Cāozuò méidiànzuàn
Operate the Electric Coal Drill

复习 Revision

连线。 Match.

螺丝

electric coal drill

煤电钻

screw

煤炭

electric coal drill switch

煤电钻开关

coal

职通中文 煤矿开采技术（初级篇）

 热身 Warm-up

下列图片你认识多少？ How many of the following pictures do you know?

zuàngǎn
钻杆
drill pipe

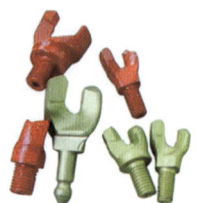
zuàntóu
钻头
drill bit

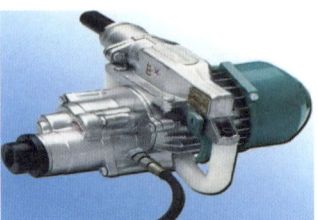
méidiànzuàn
煤电钻
electric coal drill

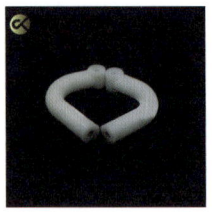
méidiànzuàn bǎshǒu
煤电钻 把手
handle of the electric coal drill

méibì
煤壁
coal wall

dǐngbǎn
顶板
roof

 学习生词 Words and Expressions 🎧 19-01

1	操作	cāozuò	v.	operate
2	安装	ānzhuāng	v.	install
3	钻杆	zuàngǎn	n.	drill pipe
4	手柄	shǒubǐng	n.	handle
5	左	zuǒ	n.	left

168

6	右	yòu	n.	right
7	站立	zhànlì	v.	stand
8	身体	shēntǐ	n.	body
9	贴	tiē	v.	keep close to
10	后面	hòumiàn	n.	rear
11	将	jiāng	prep.	used to introduce the object before the verb
12	钻头	zuàntóu	n.	drill bit
13	对准	duìzhǔn	phr.	aim at
14	打眼处	dǎyǎnchù	n.	drill point
15	角度	jiǎodù	n.	angle
16	手指	shǒuzhǐ	n.	finger
17	慢	màn	adj.	slow
18	压下	yāxia	phr.	press
19	转动	zhuàndòng	v.	rotate
20	推进	tuījìn	v.	push forward

词语练习 Word Exercises

1. 看图片，将相应的字母填在括号里。Look at the pictures and fill in the corresponding letters in the brackets.

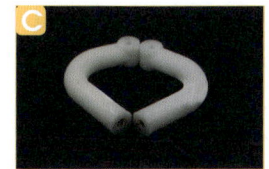

❶ 煤壁　　　　　（　　）　　❷ 煤电钻钻杆　　　（　　）

❸ 煤电钻把手　　（　　）　　❹ 煤电钻　　　　　（　　）

2. 朗读词语搭配。Read aloud the word collocations.

❶ 安装	安装钻杆	❷ 压下	压下按钮
	安装钻头		压下开关
❸ 握住	握住手柄	❹ 操作	操作煤电钻
	握住胶管口		操作采煤机

学习课文　Text　🎧 19-02

操作煤电钻
Cāozuò méidiànzuàn

安装好钻杆后，双手握住煤电钻手柄，左脚和右脚向前站立，身体贴在煤电钻后面，将钻头对准打眼处，调整好角度，用手指慢慢压下按钮，钻杆开始转动，身体均匀向前用力，操作煤电钻向前推进。

第 19 课 | 操作煤电钻

Operate the Electric Coal Drill

Install the drill pipe, hold the handle of the electric coal drill with both hands, stand with both feet facing forward. Keep your body close to the rear of the electric coal drill, aim the drill bit at the drill point, adjust the angle and slowly press the button with fingers. When the drill pipe begins to rotate, make your body move forward evenly to exert your force and operate the electric coal drill to push it forward.

课文练习 Text Exercises

1. 根据课文内容，判断对错。Tell True (T) or False (F) according to the text.

Statements	Answer	
❶ 要双手握住煤电钻手柄。	A. 是	B. 不是
❷ 身体贴在煤电钻后面，右脚（或左脚）向前站立，并将钻头对准打眼处。	A. 是	B. 不是
❸ 慢慢压下按钮，钻杆开始转动，身体用力，推进煤电钻。	A. 是	B. 不是
❹ 将钻头对准打眼处后，可以压下按钮，不再需要调整角度。	A. 是	B. 不是

2. 根据课文内容，选词填空。Choose the words to fill in the blanks according to the text.

❶ 操作煤电钻前要安装（　　　）

　A. 钻杆　　　　　　B. 把手　　　　　　C. 开关

❷ 双手握住煤电钻手柄，身体紧贴煤电钻（   ）

   A. 开关　　　　　　　　B. 后面　　　　　　　　C. 把手

❸ 左脚和右脚向前站立，将（   ）对准打眼处。

   A. 钻头　　　　　　　　B. 钻杆　　　　　　　　C. 把手

❹ 将钻头对准（   ），调整好角度，压下按钮，开始操作煤电钻。

   A. 打眼处　　　　　　　B. 开关　　　　　　　　C. 按钮

学习语法 Grammar

语法点1 Grammar Point 1

介词：将 The preposition: 将

相当于"把"。

It equals to "把".

---

❶ Jiāng shēntǐ tiē zài méidiànzuàn hòumiàn.
　将 身体 贴在 煤电钻 后面。Keep the body close to the rear of the electric coal drill.

❷ Jiāng zuàntóu tiáozhěng hǎo jiǎodù.
　将 钻头 调整 好 角度。Make the angle adjusted for the drill bit.

❸ Jiāng méidiànzuàn xiàng qián tuījìn.
　将 煤电钻 向 前 推进。Push forward the electric coal drill.

语法点1练习 Grammar Point Exercises 1

用"将"改写句子。Rewrite the sentences with "将".

❶ 瓦检仪的背带要挂在脖子上。_____

2 拧松灯泡后盖可以调整干涉条纹清晰度。_____

3 下井前要做好所有的准备工作。_____

4 应该取下自救器的保护罩。_____

语法点 2 Grammar Point 2

形容词重叠：慢慢　The reduplication of an adjective: 慢慢

表示缓慢，也指逐步，不是一下子。
It indicates being slow or gradual, not sudden.

---

1 用 手指 慢慢 压下按钮。
　Yòng shǒuzhǐ mànmàn yāxia ànniǔ.
　Slowly press the button with fingers.

2 罐笼 慢慢 运行 到 井下。
　Guànlóng mànmàn yùnxíng dào jǐngxià.
　The cage slowly runs down the shaft.

3 测风 时 慢慢 移动 行走的脚步。
　Cèfēng shí mànmàn yídòng xíngzǒu de jiǎobù.
　Walk slowly during the wind measurement.

语法点 2 练习 Grammar Point Exercises 2

连词成句。Rearrange the words to form sentences.

1 ①打开　②他　③风门　④慢慢

_____

2 ①好好　②你们　③要　④知识　⑤学习　⑥安全

_____

3 ①我们　②检查　③应该　④好好　⑤仪器

_____

汉字书写 Writing Chinese Characters

zuǒ
左

yòu
右

lìng
另

dòng
动

文化拓展 Culture Insight

The Origin of Chinese Characters

Starting around the 14th century BC, oracle bone inscriptions in the late Shang Dynasty were seen as the first form of Chinese characters, and various character forms emerged. The evolution of Chinese characters is a process of gradual standardization and stabilization of Chinese character forms and styles. The small seal script fixed the number of strokes for each character; the clerical script formed a new stroke system of gradual flat square shape; after the birth of the regular script, the form and shape of Chinese characters became stable, and the basic strokes of "horizontal stroke, vertical stroke, left-falling stroke, dot stroke, right-falling stroke, rise, and turning stroke" were determined. The shapes of strokes were further standardized, and the number and order of strokes for each character were also fixed.

第 19 课 ｜ 操作煤电钻

 小结 Summary

词语 Words

朗读下面的短语。Read aloud the following phrases.

安装钻杆	调整角度	握住手柄	压下按钮
向前用力	向前推进	操作煤电钻	对准打眼处

语法 Grammar

朗读下面的句子。Read aloud the following sentences.

1. 将身体贴在煤电钻后面。
2. 将钻头调整好角度。
3. 用手指慢慢压下按钮。
4. 你要好好学习测风的方法。

课文理解 Text Comprehension

复述课文内容。Retell the text.

　　操作煤电钻前，要先安装好_____，然后双手握住煤电钻_____，左脚和右脚_____站立，身体贴在煤电钻_____，将钻头对准_____，调整好_____，用手指慢慢压下按钮，钻杆开始_____，身体均匀向前_____，操作煤电钻向前_____。

175

第 20 课 Lesson 20

Guāntíng méidiànzuàn
关停煤电钻
Shut down the Electric Coal Drill

复习 Revision

连线。Match.

钻头		drill bit
手柄		drill pipe
钻杆		handle

热身 Warm-up

下列图片你认识多少？ How many of the following pictures do you know?

méifěn
煤粉
coal powder

zuànkǒng
钻孔
drill hole

méidiànzuàn ànniǔ
煤电钻 按钮
button of the electric coal drill

第 20 课 | 关停煤电钻

xuánzhuǎn
旋转
rotate

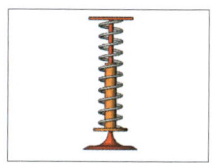
láihuí
来回
back and forth

tuījìn
推进
push forward

 学习生词 Words and Expressions 🎧 20-01

1	关停	guāntíng	v.	shut down
2	钻	zuān	v.	drill
3	要求	yāoqiú	v.	require
4	深度	shēndù	n.	depth
5	停止	tíngzhǐ	v.	stop
6	继续	jìxù	v.	continue
7	来回	láihuí	adv.	back and forth
8	拉动	lādòng	v.	pull
9	排除	páichú	v.	get rid of
10	煤粉	méifěn	n.	coal powder
11	拆下	chāixia	phr.	remove
12	切断	qiēduàn	phr.	cut off
13	电源	diànyuán	n.	power supply
14	放置	fàngzhì	v.	put

15	干燥	gānzào	*adj.*	dry
16	电缆	diànlǎn	*n.*	cable
17	并	bìng	*conj.*	and
18	收	shōu	*v.*	put

词语练习 Word Exercises

1. 看图片，将相应的字母填在括号里。Look at the pictures and fill in the corresponding letters in the brackets.

❶ 煤电钻　（　　）　❷ 煤电钻按钮（　　）　❸ 电缆　　（　　）

❹ 钻孔　　（　　）　❺ 钻杆　　　（　　）　❻ 煤粉　　（　　）

2. 选词填空。Choose the words to fill in the blanks.

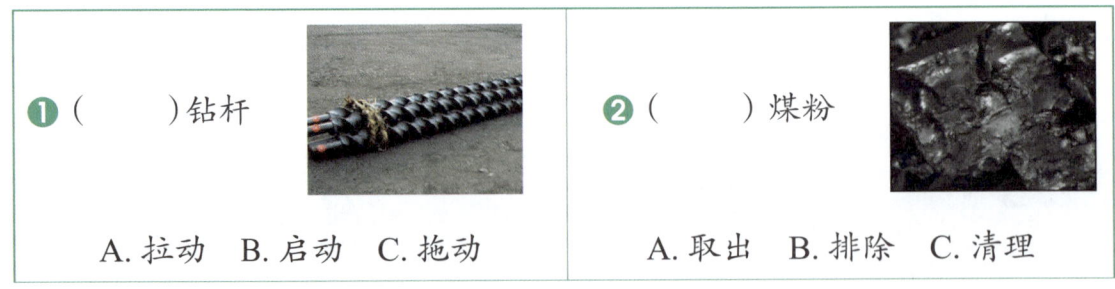

❶（　　）钻杆　　　　　　　　❷（　　）煤粉

　A. 拉动　B. 启动　C. 拖动　　　A. 取出　B. 排除　C. 清理

第20课 | 关停煤电钻

❸（　　）按钮

A. 检查　B. 松开　C. 按下

❹ 将电缆（　　）

A. 收好　B 接好　C. 放好

 **学习课文** Text 🎧 20-02

Guāntíng méidiànzuàn
关停煤电钻

Dāng méidiànzuàn zuāndào yāoqiú shēndù hòu, tíngzhǐ tuījìn,
当煤电钻钻到要求深度后，停止推进，
ràng méidiànzuàn jìxù gōngzuò, láihuí lādòng zuàngǎn, páichú méifěn,
让煤电钻继续工作，来回拉动钻杆，排除煤粉，
ránhòu sōngkāi ànniǔ, tíngzhǐ xuánzhuǎn. Qǔchū méidiànzuàn, chāixia
然后松开按钮，停止旋转。取出煤电钻，拆下
zuàngǎn, qiēduàn diànyuán, bǎ méidiànzuàn fàngzhì zài gānzào、ānquán
钻杆，切断电源，把煤电钻放置在干燥、安全
de dìdiǎn, bìng jiāng diànlǎn shōuhǎo.
的地点，并将电缆收好。

Shut down the Electric Coal Drill

When the electric coal drill reaches the required depth, stop pushing it forward and let it continue to work. Pull the drill pipe back and forth to get rid of the coal powder, then release the button and stop rotating. Take out the electric coal drill, remove the drill pipe, cut off the power supply, put the electric coal drill in a dry and safe place, and put the cable away.

课文练习 Text Exercises

1. 根据课文内容，判断对错。Tell True (T) or False (F) according to the text.

Statements	Answer
❶ 当煤电钻钻到要求深度后，停止推进。	A.是　　B.不是
❷ 当煤电钻钻到要求深度后，停止推进，让煤电钻继续工作。	A.是　　B.不是
❸ 当煤电钻钻到要求深度后，来回拉动钻杆，排除煤粉，然后松开按钮，停止旋转。	A.是　　B.不是
❹ 关停煤电钻后，拆下钻杆，将煤电钻放置在指定干燥安全的地点，并将电缆收好。	A.是　　B.不是

2. 根据课文内容，选词填空。Choose the words to fill in the blanks according to the text.

❶ 当煤电钻钻到要求深度后，停止推进，让煤电钻（　　）工作。
　A. 不再　　　　　B. 停止　　　　　C. 继续

❷ 煤电钻钻到要求深度后，（　　）按钮，停止旋转。
　A. 关闭　　　　　B. 松开　　　　　C. 按下

❸ 当煤电钻钻到要求深度后，来回拉动钻杆，排除（　　）。
　A. 粉尘　　　　　B. 灰尘　　　　　C. 煤粉

❹ 当煤电钻钻到要求深度后，拆下钻杆，将煤电钻放置在（　　）、安全的地点，并将电缆收好。
　A. 通风　　　　　B. 潮湿　　　　　C. 干燥

第20课 | 关停煤电钻

学习语法 Grammar

语法点 1　Grammar Point 1

副词：来回　The adverb: 来回

表示重复相同动作。
It indicates repeating the same action.

① Láihuí lādòng zuàngǎn, páichú méifěn.
　来回拉动钻杆，排除煤粉。Pull the drill pipe back and forth to get rid of the coal powder.

② Gōngzuòchē zài chējiān láihuí pǎo.
　工作车在车间来回跑。The work vehicle runs in the workshop back and forth.

③ Gōngrén láihuí tiáozhěng zuàntóu de jiǎodù.
　工人来回调整钻头的角度。The workers adjust the angle of the drill bit again and again.

语法点 1 练习　Grammar Point Exercises 1

连词成句。Rearrange the words to form sentences.

① ①检查　②矿灯　③来回　④工人　⑤灯头　⑥的

_____

② ①来回　②后盖　③不要　④拧　⑤的　⑥电池

_____

③ ①他　②调整　③钻头　④来回　⑤的　⑥角度

_____

④ ①拉动　②通过　③排除　④来回　⑤钻杆　⑥煤粉

_____

181

语法点 2 Grammar Point 2

连词：并 The conjunction: 并

表示几个动作同时进行或几种性质同时存在。
It indicates that several actions are performed simultaneously or several properties exist simultaneously.

1. Bǎ méidiànzuàn fàng zài gānzào、ānquán de dìdiǎn, bìng jiāng diànlǎn shōuhǎo.
   把煤电钻放在干燥、安全的地点，并将电缆收好。Put the electric coal drill in a dry and safe place and put the cable away.

2. Jiāng zuàntóu duìzhǔn dǎyǎnchù, bìng tiáozhěng hǎo jiǎodù.
   将钻头对准打眼处，并调整好角度。Aim the drill bit at the drill point and adjust the angle.

3. Tóngshí guānbì fēngbiǎo hé miǎobiǎo de kāiguān, bìng dúchū fēngbiǎo de dúshù.
   同时关闭风表和秒表的开关，并读出风表的读数。Turn off the switches of the anemometer and of the stopwatch simultaneously and read out the data on the anemometer.

语法点 2 练习 Grammar Point Exercises 2

用"并"完成句子。Complete the sentences with "并".

1. 下井前要穿好工作服，_____。

2. 双手抓住猴车的吊杆，_____。

3. 乘坐罐笼要依次进入，_____。

4. 井下行走时要走人行道，_____。

第20课 | 关停煤电钻

汉字书写 Writing Chinese Characters

职业拓展 Career Insight

Treatment of Abnormalities in the Electric Coal Drill

When the temperature of the shell of the electric coal drill is abnormal (exceeding 60°C), shut it down and let it cool before use. When there is abnormal sound of the electric coal drill or other abnormal situations, shut it down immediately and cut off the power supply for inspection and treatment. When handling the electric coal drill, carry it with hands or shoulders, do not drag it on the ground.

 小结 Summary

词语 Words

朗读下面的短语。Read aloud the following phrases.

停止推进	停止旋转	拆下钻杆	切断电源
收好电缆	松开按钮	排除煤粉	拉动钻杆
继续工作	来回拉动		

语法 Grammar

朗读下面的句子。Read aloud the following sentences.

1. 来回拉动钻杆,排除煤粉。
2. 工人来回调整钻头的角度。
3. 把煤电钻放在干燥、安全的地点,并将电缆收好。
4. 将钻头对准打眼处,并调整好角度。

课文理解 Text Comprehension

根据课文内容,判断对错。Tell True (T) or False (F) according to the text.

当煤电钻钻进到要求深度后,停止推进。	A. 是	B. 不是
取出煤电钻后,不需要拆下钻杆。	A. 是	B. 不是
将煤电钻放置在干燥、安全的地点。	A. 是	B. 不是
当煤电钻钻到要求深度后,让煤电钻继续工作。	A. 是	B. 不是

第 21 课 Lesson 21

Zhuāng léiguǎn
装雷管
Install the Blasting Cap

 复习 Revision

连线。Match.

煤粉		cable
电源		drill pipe
煤电钻按钮		power supply
钻杆		button of the electric coal drill
电缆		electric coal drill
煤电钻		coal powder

热身 Warm-up

下列图片你认识多少？ How many of the following pictures do you know?

zhàyàojuǎn
炸药卷
explosive cartridge

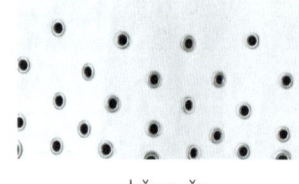

kǒngyǎn
孔眼
hole

diàn
电
electricity

jiǎoxiàn
脚线
foot line

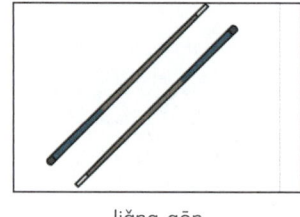

liǎng gēn
两　根
two

kǔn
捆
bind

学习生词 Words and Expressions 🎧 21-01

1	雷管	léiguǎn	n.	blasting cap
2	炸药卷	zhàyàojuǎn	n.	explosive cartridge
3	顶端	dǐngduān	n.	top
4	扎	zhā	v.	make (a hole)
5	孔眼	kǒngyǎn	n.	hole
6	插入	chārù	phr.	insert
7	剩余	shèngyú	v.	(of sb./sth.) be leftover

8	脚线	jiǎoxiàn	n.	foot line
9	缠	chán	v.	wrap
10	根	gēn	m.	a measure word
11	连接	liánjiē	v.	connect
12	起来	qǐlái	v.	used after a verb to indicate the commencement and continuation of an action
13	只	zhǐ	adv.	only
14	装	zhuāng	v.	hold, load
15	斜插	xiéchā	phr.	insert diagonally
16	或者	huòzhě	conj.	or
17	捆	kǔn	v.	bind

词语练习 Word Exercises

1. 连线。Match.

脚线   electricity

孔眼   explosive cartridge

炸药卷   foot line

电   hole

2. 朗读词语搭配。Read aloud the word collocations.

❶	安装	安装雷管	❷	插入	插入孔眼
		安装炸药			插入鼻孔
❸	一个	一个孔眼	❹	电	电雷管
		一个雷管			电矿灯

学习课文 Text 🎧 21-02

Ānzhuāng léiguǎn
安装 雷管

Ānzhuāng léiguǎn shí, xiān zài zhàyàojuǎn de dǐngduān zhā yí gè
安装雷管时，先在炸药卷的顶端扎一个
kǒngyǎn, bǎ diànléiguǎn chārù kǒngyǎn, ránhòu bǎ shèngyú de jiǎoxiàn
孔眼，把电雷管插入孔眼，然后把剩余的脚线
chán zài zhàyàojuǎn shang, zuìhòu bǎ liǎng gēn jiǎoxiàn liánjiē qilai. Yí
缠在炸药卷上，最后把两根脚线连接起来。一
gè zhàyàojuǎn zhǐ néng zhuāng yí gè léiguǎn, yánjìn jiāng diànléiguǎn
个炸药卷只能装一个雷管，严禁将电雷管
xiéchā zài zhàyàojuǎn shang huòzhě kǔn zài zhàyàojuǎn shang.
斜插在炸药卷上或者捆在炸药卷上。

Install the Blasting Cap

When installing the blasting cap, make a hole at the top of the explosive cartridge, insert the electric blasting cap into the hole, and then wrap the remaining foot line around the explosive cartridge, and finally connect the two foot lines together. One explosive cartridge can only hold one blasting cap; do not insert the electric blasting cap diagonally into the explosive cartridge or bind it to the explosive cartridge.

课文练习 Text Exercises

1. 根据课文内容，判断对错。Tell True (T) or False (F) according to the text.

Statements	Answer
❶ 装雷管时，先在炸药卷的顶端扎一个孔眼。	A. 是　　B. 不是
❷ 一个炸药卷只能装一个雷管。	A. 是　　B. 不是
❸ 严禁将电雷管斜插在炸药卷上。	A. 是　　B. 不是
❹ 严禁将电雷管捆在炸药卷上。	A. 是　　B. 不是

2. 根据课文内容，选词填空。Choose the words to fill in the blanks according to the text.

❶ 装_____时，先在_____的顶端扎一个孔眼。　　A. 雷管　　B. 炸药卷

❷ 剩余的_____缠在炸药卷上。　　A. 炸药卷　　B. 脚线

❸ _____炸药卷只能装一个_____。　　A. 一个　　B. 雷管

❹ _____将电雷管_____在炸药卷上。　　A. 严禁　　B. 斜插

学习语法 Grammar

语法点 1 Grammar Point 1

趋向补语：起来　The complement of direction: 起来

用在动词后，可以表示人或事物合在一起。

It is used after a verb to indicate that people or things are together.

> Bǎ liǎng gēn jiǎoxiàn liánjiē qilai.
> ① 把 两 根 脚线 连接 起来。Connect the two foot lines.
>
> Bǎ liǎng gēn diànxiàn liánjiē qilai.
> ② 把 两 根 电线 连接 起来。Connect the two wires.
>
> Bǎ liǎng tiáo lù liánjiē qilai.
> ③ 把 两 条 路 连接 起来。Connect the two roads.

语法点1练习 Grammar Point Exercises 1

选词填空。Choose the words to fill in the blanks.

A. 起来   B. 出来

① 把你的名字写_____。

② 工人们开掘_____一条巷道。

③ 两条电线应该连接_____。

④ 我们要把两条路连接_____。

语法点2 Grammar Point 2

> **连词：或者**   The conjunction: 或者
>
> 用于表示选择关系。常用结构为"或者A或者B，A或者B"。
> It is used to indicate a relationship of choice. The common structure is "或者A或者B, A或者B".
>
> ---
>
> Diànléiguǎn bù néng xiéchā zài huòzhě kǔn zài zhàyàojuǎn shang.
> ① 电雷管 不能 斜插 在 或者 捆在 炸药卷 上。Do not insert the electric blasting cap diagonally into the explosive cartridge or bind it to the explosive cartridge.
>
> Nǐ kěyǐ shuō huòzhě xiě.
> ② 你可以说 或者 写。You can say or write it.
>
> Niē xīqìqiú 5 cì huòzhě 6 cì.
> ③ 捏吸气球 5 次或者 6 次。Squeeze the suction balloon 5 or 6 times.

第21课 | 装雷管

语法点2练习 Grammar Point Exercises 2

用"或者"完成句子。Complete the sentences with "或者".

1. 我要吃_____。
2. 我要去_____。
3. 巷道的形状可以是_____。
4. 电雷管不能_____炸药卷上。

汉字书写 Writing Chinese Characters

rèn 认 认 认 认
认 认 认 认 认

bā 巴 巴 巴 巴
巴 巴 巴 巴 巴

ràng 让 让 让 让 让
让 让 让 让 让

bǎ 把 把 把 把 把 把 把
把 把 把 把 把

文化拓展 Culture Insight

Lantern-Making

In ancient times, when the Mid-Autumn Festival was around the corner, children used bamboo paper to make bunny lanterns, peach lanterns, or square lanterns with their parents' help. In addition, many children also used fruit peels to make lanterns. They also presented papaya lanterns, banana lanterns, etc. The simplest ones were the "pomelo peel lanterns", which can be made by almost every child in every household. The lanterns made could be used to celebrate the Mid-Autumn Festival by tying them to bamboo poles, tiled eaves, terraces and other high places, and could also be used for couples to enjoy the moon while holding the lanterns.

小结 Summary

词语 Words

根据课文内容，选择恰当的词语。Choose the appropriate words according to the text.

安装雷管时，先在_____的顶端扎一个孔眼，把_____插入孔眼，然后把剩余的脚线_____在炸药卷上，最后把两根_____连接起来。

A. 脚线　　　　B. 炸药卷　　　　C. 电雷管　　　　D. 缠

语法 Grammar

朗读下面的句子。Read aloud the following sentences.

1. 把两根脚线连接起来。

2. 把两根电线连接起来。

3. 电雷管不能斜插在或者捆在炸药卷上。

4. 用手捏吸气球 5 次或者 6 次。

第 21 课 ｜ 装雷管

课文理解 Text Comprehension

复述课文内容。**Retell the text.**

安装雷管时，先在炸药卷的＿＿＿＿扎一个＿＿＿＿，把电雷管插入孔眼，然后把剩余的＿＿＿＿缠在炸药卷上，最后把两根脚线＿＿＿＿起来。一个炸药卷只能装一个＿＿＿＿，严禁将电雷管＿＿＿＿在炸药卷上或者＿＿＿＿在炸药卷上。

第 22 课 Lesson 22

Zhuāng zhàyào
装炸药
Load Explosives

复习 Revision

连线。Match.

中文	图片	English
孔眼		foot line
炸药卷		explosive cartridge
脚线		hole
电		bind
捆		electricity
两根		two

194

 第22课 | 装炸药

热身 Warm-up

下列图片你认识多少？ How many of the following pictures do you know?

pàoní
炮泥
stemming

pàokǒng
炮孔
blast hole

zhàyào
炸药
explosives

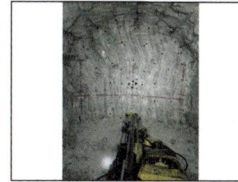
léiguǎn
雷管
blasting cap

ānquán
安全
safety

pàogùn
炮棍
tamping bar

 学习生词 Words and Expressions  22-01

1	炸药	zhàyào	n.	explosive
2	炮棍	pàogùn	n.	tamping bar
3	药卷	yàojuǎn	n.	explosive cartridge
4	轻	qīng	adj.	gentle
5	推入	tuīrù	phr.	push into
6	底部	dǐbù	n.	bottom

7	紧密	jǐnmì	*adj.*	close
8	接触	jiēchù	*v.*	contact
9	炮泥	pàoní	*n.*	stemming
10	填满	tiánmǎn	*phr.*	fill to the full
11	炮孔	pàokǒng	*n.*	blast hole
12	装填	zhuāngtián	*v.*	load
13	填	tián	*v.*	fill
14	缓慢	huǎnmàn	*adj.*	slow
15	捣实	dǎoshí	*phr.*	make firm by ramming
16	用力	yònglì	*v.*	exert oneself
17	过猛	guò měng	*phr.*	excessive force
18	过期	guòqī	*v.*	be expired

词语练习 Word Exercises

1. 选词填空。Choose the words to fill in the blanks.

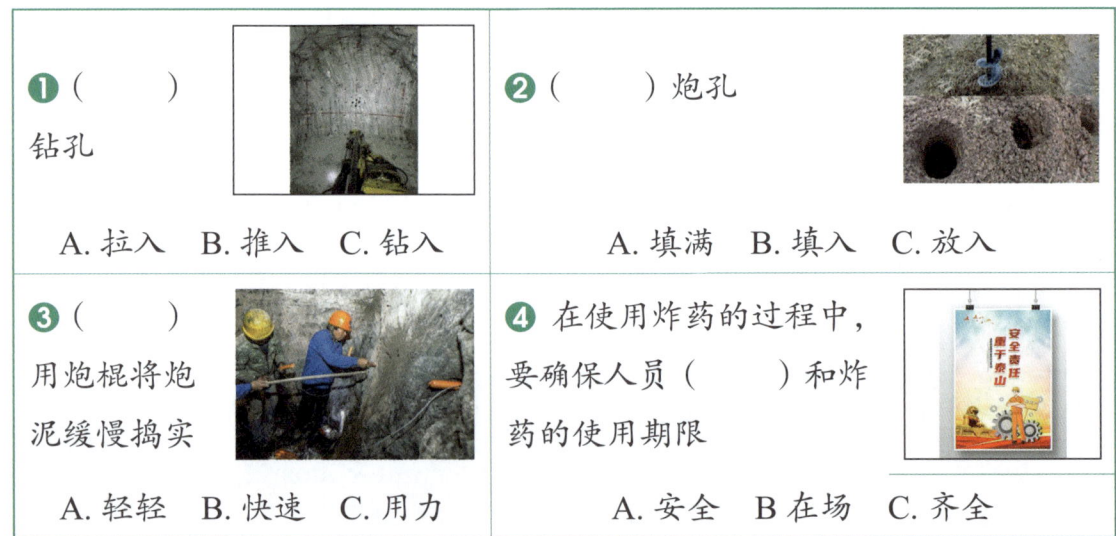

❶ （   ）钻孔

　A. 拉入　B. 推入　C. 钻入

❷ （   ）炮孔

　A. 填满　B. 填入　C. 放入

❸ （   ）用炮棍将炮泥缓慢捣实

　A. 轻轻　B. 快速　C. 用力

❹ 在使用炸药的过程中，要确保人员（   ）和炸药的使用期限

　A. 安全　B. 在场　C. 齐全

第 22 课 | 装炸药

2. 看图片，将相应的字母填在括号里。Look at the pictures and fill in the corresponding letters in the brackets.

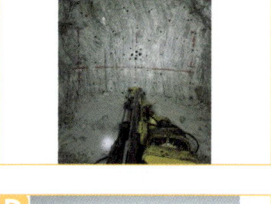

1 炮棍　　（　　）　　2 炮孔　　（　　）　　3 炸药　　（　　）
4 安全　　（　　）　　5 炮泥　　（　　）　　6 雷管　　（　　）

 学习课文　Text　🎧 22-02

Zhuāng zhàyào
装 炸药

　　Zhuāng zhàyào shí, xiān yòng pàogùn jiāng yàojuǎn qīngqīng tuīrù zuànkǒng dǐbù, shǐ yàojuǎn hé zuànkǒng dǐbù jǐnmì jiēchù. Zài yòng pàoní tiánmǎn pàokǒng. Zhuāngtián shí yào yì shǒu lā jiǎoxiàn, yì shǒu tián pàoní, qīngqīng yòng pàogùn jiāng pàoní huǎnmàn dǎoshí, bù néng yònglì guò měng.

　　装炸药时，先用炮棍将药卷轻轻推入钻孔底部，使药卷和钻孔底部紧密接触。再用炮泥填满炮孔。装填时要一手拉脚线，一手填炮泥，轻轻用炮棍将炮泥缓慢捣实，不能用力过猛。

Zài shǐyòng zhàyào de guòchéng zhōng, yào quèbǎo rényuán de ānquán, jìnzhǐ shǐyòng guòqī zhàyào.

在使用炸药的过程中，要确保人员的安全，禁止使用过期炸药。

Load Explosives

When loading explosives, first gently push the explosive cartridge with a tamping bar to the bottom of the drill hole, making the explosive cartridge in close contact with the bottom of the drill hole. Fill the blast hole to the full with the stemming. During the loading process, pull the foot line with one hand and fill the stemming with the other hand. Gently use the tamping bar to slowly compact the stemming, and overexertion is prohibited. In the process of using explosives, remember to ensure the personnel safety and do not use expired explosives.

课文练习 Text Exercises

1. 根据课文内容，判断对错。Tell True (T) or False (F) according to the text.

Statements	Answer
① 装炸药时先用炮棍将药卷轻轻推入钻孔底部。	A. 是　　B. 不是
② 用力将炮泥缓慢捣实。	A. 是　　B. 不是
③ 装炸药不能用力过猛。	A. 是　　B. 不是
④ 在使用炸药的过程中，要确保人员的安全和炸药的使用期限。	A. 是　　B. 不是

2. 根据课文内容，选词填空。Choose the words to fill in the blanks according to the text.

① 装炸药时先用（　　）将药卷轻轻推入钻孔底部。
A. 炮泥　　　　　B. 炮棍　　　　　C. 脚线

② 再用（　　）填满炮孔。装填时要一手拉脚线，一手填炮泥。
A. 炮泥　　　　　B. 脚线　　　　　C. 炮棍

③ 装炸药时要（　　）用炮棍将炮泥缓慢捣实，不能用力过猛。
A. 缓慢　　　　　B. 用力　　　　　C. 轻轻

④ 在使用炸药的过程中，要确保人员的（　　），禁止使用过期炸药。
A. 全勤　　　　　B. 安全　　　　　C. 平安

 学习语法 Grammar

 语法点1 Grammar Point 1

动词：使　The verb: 使
表示致使产生一定的结果。
It indicates causing a certain result.

① Shǐ yàojuǎn hé zuànkǒng dǐbù jǐnmì jiēchù.
使 药卷和 钻孔底部紧密接触。Make the explosive cartridge in close contact with the bottom of the drill hole.

② Shǐ fēngbiǎo bǎochí chuízhí yú fēngliú de fāngxiàng.
使 风表 保持垂直于风流的方向。Keep the anemometer vertical to the direction of the wind flow.

③ Yāxia ànniǔ shǐ zuàngǎn kāishǐ zhuàndòng.
压下按钮使 钻杆 开始 转动。Press the button to make the drill pipe rotate.

语法点1练习 Grammar Point Exercises 1

连词成句。Rearrange the words to form sentences.

1. ①两根 ②连接 ③使 ④脚线 ⑤起来

   _____

2. ①使 ②停止 ③煤电钻 ④旋转

   _____

3. ①同时 ②风门 ③通过 ④使 ⑤人员 ⑥所有

   _____

4. ①风表 ②使 ③回零 ④的 ⑤指针

   _____

语法点2 Grammar Point 2

固定格式：在……（的）过程中 The fixed pattern: 在……（的）过程中

表示"在动作进行期间"的意义。
It indicates "during the process of an ongoing action".

1. Zài shǐyòng zhàyào de guòchéng zhōng yào quèbǎo rényuán de ānquán.
   在使用炸药的过程中要确保人员的安全。In the process of using explosives, ensure the personnel safety.

2. Zài cè fēng de guòchéng zhōng yào ràng fēngbiǎo kōngzhuàn 30 miǎo.
   在测风的过程中要让风表空转30秒。In the process of the anemometry work, let the anemometer idle for 30 seconds.

3. Zài chéngzuò guànlóng de guòchéng zhōng bù kěyǐ wánshuǎ、dǎnào.
   在乘坐罐笼的过程中不可以玩耍、打闹。In the process of riding the cage, playing or being rowdy is not allowed.

第22课 ｜ 装炸药

语法点 2 练习 Grammar Point Exercises 2

完成句子。Complete the sentences.

1. 在学习的过程中，要_____。
2. 在测风的过程中，要_____。
3. 在检查瓦检仪光路的过程中，要_____。
4. 在操作煤电钻的过程中，要_____。

汉字书写 Writing Chinese Characters

yòng　用 用 用 用 用
用

shuǎi　甩 甩 甩 甩 甩
甩

zé　则 则 则 则 则 则
则

cè　测 测 测 测 测 测 测 测 测
测

职业拓展 Career Insight

Explosives

Explosives are substances that can burn violently (i.e. explode) in a very short period of time, and also substances that explode with their own energy under certain external energy. In general, explosives have stable chemical and physical properties. As long as there is strong energy (provided by the primary explosive) excitation, they will explode to the outside, regardless of whether the environment is sealed, what the amount of explosives is, or even whether there is zero oxygen supply from the outside. When explosives explode, they can release a large amount of thermal energy and produce high-temperature and high-pressure gases, which can cause damage, compression, and other effects on surrounding substances.

小结 Summary

词语 Words

朗读下面的短语。Read aloud the following phrases.

推入底部　　填满炮孔　　确保安全　　轻轻推入　　缓慢捣实

紧密接触　　拉脚线　　　填炮泥　　　禁止使用

语法 Grammar

朗读下面的句子。Read aloud the following sentences.

1. 使药卷和钻孔底部紧密接触。
2. 压下按钮，使钻杆开始转动。
3. 在使用炸药的过程中，要确保人员安全。
4. 在测风的过程中，要让风表空转30秒。

第22课 | 装炸药

课文理解 Text Comprehension

根据课文内容，判断对错。Tell True (T) or False (F) according to the text.

在使用炸药的过程中，要确保人员的安全。	A. 是	B. 不是
装填时要一手拉脚线，一手填炮泥，轻轻用炮棍将炮泥缓慢捣实，不能用力过猛。	A. 是	B. 不是
装炸药时先用炮棍将药卷轻轻地推入钻孔底部，使药卷和钻孔底部紧密接触。	A. 是	B. 不是
在使用炸药的过程中，要严禁使用过期的炸药。	A. 是	B. 不是

第 23 课 Lesson 23
Liánxiàn 连线 Connection

 **复习 Revision**

连线。Match.

炸药	léiguǎn	explosives
脚线	zhàyào	foot line
雷管	zhàyàojuǎn	blasting cap
炸药卷	jiǎoxiàn	explosive cartridge

 **热身 Warm-up**

下列图片你认识多少？ How many of the following pictures do you know?

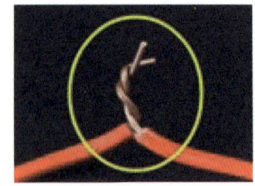   

jiētóu	bàopò	xuánkōng	qièjì
接头	爆破	悬空	切记
joint	blast	suspend	remember

学习生词 Words and Expressions 🎧 23-01

1	连线	lián//xiàn	*v.*	connect
2	完成	wánchéng	*v.*	complete
3	母线	mǔxiàn	*n.*	busbar
4	切记	qièjì	*v.*	remember
5	接头	jiētóu	*n.*	joint
6	都	dōu	*adv.*	all
7	悬空	xuánkōng	*v.*	suspend in the mid-air
8	任何	rènhé	*pron.*	any
9	物体	wùtǐ	*n.*	object
10	每	měi	*pron.*	each
11	爆破	bàopò	*v.*	blast
12	及时	jíshí	*adv.*	in time
13	收起	shōuqǐ	*phr.*	put in a proper place
14	务必	wùbì	*adv.*	be sure to
15	认真	rènzhēn	*adj.*	careful
16	执行	zhíxíng	*v.*	conduct, carry out
17	有效	yǒuxiào	*v.*	be effective

词语练习 Word Exercises

1. 看图片，将相应的字母填在括号里。Look at the pictures and fill in the corresponding letters in the brackets.

① 连线　（　）　② 母线　（　）　③ 爆破　（　）

④ 切记　（　）　⑤ 接头　（　）　⑥ 悬空　（　）

2. 朗读词语搭配。Read aloud the word collocations.

① 切记	切记注意安全	② 及时	及时上班
	切记注意危险		及时下班
③ 悬空	悬空物体	④ 认真执行	认真执行规定
	悬空设备		认真执行纪律

学习课文　Text　🎧 23-02

Liánxiàn
连线

Liánxiàn shí, shǒuxiān àn shùnxù liánjiē léiguǎn de liǎng gēn
连线时，首先按顺序连接雷管的两根

jiǎoxiàn, liánjiē wánchéng hòu, zài bǎ mǔxiàn yǔ shèngyú de liǎng gēn
脚线，连接完成后，再把母线与剩余的两根

jiǎoxiàn liánjiē. Qièjì suǒyǒu de jiētóu dōu bìxū xuánkōng, bùdé
脚线连接。切记所有的接头都必须悬空，不得

yǔ rènhé wùtǐ jiēchù. Měi cì bàopò wánchéng hòu dōu yào jíshí
与任何物体接触。每次爆破完成后都要及时

bǎ mǔxiàn shōu qǐlai. Qǐng wùbì rènzhēn zhíxíng, quèbǎo cāozuò de
把母线收起来。请务必认真执行，确保操作的

ānquán hé xiàoyǒu.
安全和有效。

Connection

When connecting, first connect the two foot lines of the blasting cap in order, and then connect the busbar to the remaining two foot lines after completing the connection. Remember that all the joints must be suspended and must not come into contact with any object. After each blasting is completed, always retract the busbar in time. Be sure to conduct it carefully to ensure the safety and effectiveness of the operation.

课文练习 Text Exercises

1. 根据课文内容，判断对错。Tell True (T) or False (F) according to the text.

Statements	Answer
❶ 首先按顺序连接雷管的两根脚线。	A. 是　　B. 不是
❷ 母线与剩余的两条脚线连接。	A. 是　　B. 不是
❸ 连线的接头都必须悬空。	A. 是　　B. 不是
❹ 爆破完成后不需要把母线收起。	A. 是　　B. 不是

2. 根据课文内容，选词填空。Choose the words to fill in the blanks according to the text.

① 首先按顺序连接雷管的两根_____。　　A. 脚线　　B. 母线

② _____与剩余的两条脚线连接。　　　　A. 脚线　　B. 母线

③ 连线的_____都必须悬空。　　　　　　A. 接头　　B. 母线

④ 每次爆破完成后需要及时把_____收起。A. 脚线　　B. 母线

学习语法 Grammar

语法点 1 Grammar Point 1

介词：按　The preposition: 按

用于引出动作行为的凭借、依据。也说"按照（zhào）"。常用结构为"按 + 名词 + 动词性成分"。

It is used to introduce the basis for an action or behavior. "按照（zhào）" can also be used. The common structure is "按 + noun + verbal element".

Àn shùnxù liánjiē léiguǎn de liǎng gēn jiǎoxiàn.
① 按顺序连接雷管的两根脚线。Connect the two foot lines of the blasting cap in order.

Àn bùzhòu jiǎnchá wǎsī qìtǐ nóngdù.
② 按步骤检查瓦斯气体浓度。Check the gas concentration following the steps.

语法点 1 练习 Grammar Point Exercises 1

选词填空。Choose the words to fill in the blanks.

　　　　　　　　A. 按　　B. 由

① 你必须_____操作步骤检查瓦检仪气密性。

2. 煤矿是_____巷道、设备和工作面组成的。

3. 乘坐罐笼时，要_____顺序依次进入。

4. 煤炭_____工人通过巷道运输出来。

语法点 2 Grammar Point 2

副词：都　The adverb: 都

表示总括。除疑问句外，所总括的成分放在"都"前。

It indicates summing up. The summarized components come before "都" except in the case of a question.

1. Suǒyǒu de jiētóu dōu bìxū xuánkōng.
   所有的接头都必须悬空。 All the joints must be suspended.

2. Měi cì bàopò wánchéng hòu, dōu yào jíshí bǎ mǔxiàn shōu qǐlái.
   每次爆破完成后，都要及时把母线收起来。 After each blasting is completed, always retract the busbar in time.

语法点 2 练习 Grammar Point Exercises 2

把"都"放在合适的位置。Put "都" in the appropriate positions.

1. A 为了下井 B 煤矿工人 C 必须取得 D 合格证。

2. 我们 A 的 B 矿灯 C 没有 D 问题。

3. A 风表和 B 秒表 C 要关闭 D。

4. 把剩余的 A 脚线 B 缠在 C 炸药卷 D 上。

 汉字书写 Writing Chinese Characters

 文化拓展 Culture Insight

Mid-Autumn Festival

On Mid-Autumn Festival, the moon becomes big and round on the clear night. Do you know the customs of Mid-Autumn Festival? Let me tell you about that. Mid-Autumn Festival falls on the 15th day of the eighth lunar month. It is a must to offer sacrifices to the moon, admire the full moon and eat moon cakes on the festival. People also enjoy the "reunion dinner" together with their families, that's why Mid-Autumn Festival is also called the "Reunion Day".

小结 Summary

词语 Words

根据课文内容，选择恰当的词语。Choose the appropriate words according to the text.

切记所有的_____都必须悬空，不得与任何物体_____。每次爆破完成后都要及时把_____收起来。请务必认真执行，确保操作的安全和_____。

A. 接触　　　B. 母线　　　C. 有效　　　D. 接头

语法 Grammar

朗读下面的句子。Read aloud the following sentences.

1. 按顺序连接雷管的两根脚线。
2. 按步骤检查瓦斯气体浓度。
3. 所有的接头都必须悬空。
4. 每次爆破完成后都要及时把母线收起来。

课文理解 Text Comprehension

根据课文内容，判断对错。Tell True (T) or False (F) according to the text.

首先按顺序连接雷管的两根脚线。	A. 是	B. 不是
母线与剩余的两根脚线连接。	A. 是	B. 不是
连线的接头都必须悬空。	A. 是	B. 不是
爆破完成后不需要把母线收起。	A. 是	B. 不是

211

第 24 课 Lesson 24

Qǐbào
起爆
Detonation

 复习 Revision

连线。Match.

悬空		remember
切记		suspend in the mid-air
母线		joint
接头	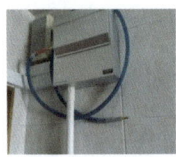	busbar
爆破		blast

第 24 课 | 起爆

热身 Warm-up

下列图片你认识多少？How many of the following pictures do you know?

yàoshi
钥匙
key

chōngdiàn
充电
charge

tíxǐng
提醒
remind

fābàoqì
发爆器
detonator

学习生词 Words and Expressions 🎧 24-01

1	起爆	qǐbào	v.	detonate
2	准确	zhǔnquè	adj.	accurate
3	发爆器	fābàoqì	n.	detonator
4	接线端	jiēxiànduān	n.	wiring terminal
5	钥匙	yàoshi	n.	key
6	至	zhì	v.	to
7	充电	chōng//diàn	v.	charge
8	报警	bào//jǐng	v.	sound the alarm
9	发出	fāchū	v.	produce (sound, etc.)
10	爆破警报	bàopò jǐngbào	phr.	blasting alarm
11	提醒	tí//xǐng	v.	remind

213

12	周围	zhōuwéi	n.	the space all round
13	人们	rénmen	n.	people
14	等待	děngdài	v.	wait
15	转回	zhuǎnhuí	phr.	turn back
16	放电	fàng//diàn	v.	discharge
17	通电起爆	tōngdiàn qǐbào	phr.	power on and then detonate

词语练习 Word Exercises

1. 看图片，将相应的字母填在括号里。Look at the pictures and fill in the corresponding letters in the brackets.

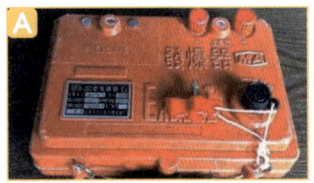

1 转回　　　　　　　（　） 2 充电　　　　　　　（　）

3 提醒　　　　　　　（　） 4 发爆器　　　　　　（　）

5 钥匙　　　　　　　（　） 6 报警　　　　　　　（　）

2. 朗读词语搭配。Read aloud the word collocations.

❶ 回	转回钥匙	❷ 提醒	提醒人们
	转回手把		提醒工人
❸ 警报	爆破警报	❹ 等待	等待5秒
	安全警报		等待救援

学习课文 Text 24-02

Qǐbào
起爆

1. Bǎ mǔxiàn zhǔnquè liánjiē zài fābàoqì de jiēxiànduān.
   把母线准确连接在发爆器的接线端。

2. Bǎ yàoshi chārù fābàoqì, bìng zhuàndòng zhì chōngdiàn wèizhì.
   把钥匙插入发爆器，并转动至充电位置。

3. Dāng chōngdiàn wánchéng hòu, ànxia bàojǐng ànniǔ, fāchū bàopò jǐngbào, tíxǐng zhōuwéi rénmen zhùyì.
   当充电完成后，按下报警按钮，发出爆破警报，提醒周围人们注意。

4. Děngdài 5 miǎo hòu, zhuǎnhuí yàoshi zhì fàngdiàn wèizhì.
   等待5秒后，转回钥匙至放电位置。

5. Tōngdiàn qǐbào.
   通电起爆。

Detonation

1. Accurately connect the busbar to the wiring terminal of the detonator.

2. Insert the key into the detonator and turn it to the charging position.

3. After completing the charging, press the alarm button to issue a blasting alarm as a reminder to the people nearby.

4. Turn the key back to the discharge position after waiting for 5 seconds.

5. Power on and then detonate.

课文练习 Text Exercises

1. 根据课文内容，判断对错。Tell True (T) or False (F) according to the text.

Statements	Answer
❶ 把母线准确接在发爆器的接线端。	A. 是　　B. 不是
❷ 钥匙插入发爆器后，转动至充电位置。	A. 是　　B. 不是
❸ 充电完成后发出爆破警报，提醒周围注意安全。	A. 是　　B. 不是
❹ 等待5秒后，转回钥匙至放电位置，通电起爆。	A. 是　　B. 不是

2. 根据课文内容，选词填空。Choose the words to fill in the blanks according to the text.

❶ 把_____准确接在发爆器的接线端。

A. 脚线　　　　　　　　B. 母线

❷ 钥匙插入发爆器后，转动至_____位置。

A. 充电　　　　　　　　B. 放电

3 充电完成后，_____提醒周围人们注意安全。

　A. 警报　　　　　　B. 信号

4 等待5秒后，转回钥匙至_____位置，通电起爆。

　A. 充电　　　　　　B. 放电

学习语法 Grammar

语法点1 Grammar Point 1

动词 + 至 + 地点　Verb + 至 + place

用于表示移动的终点。多用于书面语，口语中常说"动词 + 到 + 地点"。

It is mostly used in written Chinese to indicate the destination of a movement. In spoken Chinese, "verb + 到 + place" is commonly used.

1 　Bǎ yàoshi zhuàndòng zhì chōngdiàn wèizhì.
　把 钥匙 转动 至 充电 位置。Turn the key to the charging position.

2 　Kāicǎi shèbèi yào yùnshū zhì jǐngxià.
　开采 设备 要 运输 至 井下。Mining equipment needs to be transported to the downhole.

3 　Yòng pàogùn jiāng yàojuǎn qīngqīng tuī zhì zuànkǒng dǐbù.
　用 炮棍 将 药卷 轻轻 推 至 钻孔 底部。Gently push the explosive cartridge with a tamping bar to the bottom of the drill hole.

语法点1练习 Grammar Point Exercises 1

连词成句。Rearrange the words to form sentences.

1 ①要　②罐笼　③至　④运行　⑤煤矿　⑥底部

2 ①煤电钻　②至　③位置　④充电　⑤放　⑥把

_____

3 ①药卷　②至　③推　④应该　⑤底部　⑥钻孔

_____

4 ①将　②仪器　③购买　④的　⑤至　⑥运输　⑦仓库

语法点 2　Grammar Point 2

动词 + 回　Verb + 回

表示人或事物随动作从别处到原处。

It indicates that somebody or something moves from another place to the original place.

1 Bǎ yàoshi zhuǎnhuí zhì fàngdiàn wèizhì.
把钥匙 转回 至 放电 位置。Turn the key to the discharge position.

2 Kāicǎi shèbèi yùnhuí cāngkù.
开采设备运回 仓库。Transport the mining equipment back to the warehouse.

3 Tā cóng jǐngxià dàihuí liǎng gè kuàngdēng.
他 从 井下 带回 两个 矿灯。He brought back two miner's lamps from the downhole.

语法点 2 练习　Grammar Point Exercises 2

选词填空。Choose the words to fill in the blanks.

A. 回　　B. 出

1 观察目镜和微读数视窗，读_____数据。

2 等待5秒后，把钥匙转_____放电位置。

3 职工们买_____10条毛巾。

4 请写_____起爆的步骤。

 汉字书写 Writing Chinese Characters

 职业拓展 Career Insight

The Function of the Coal Mining Machine

The coal mining machine is an important equipment for the mechanization and modernization of coal mine production. It implements a working mechanism to break coal from the coal body (coal breaking) and load it into the coal mining machine of the working face conveyor (coal loading). The coal mining machine moves at the set traction speed (traction) to ensure continuous coal breaking and coal loading processes.

小结 Summary

词语 Words

根据课文内容，选择恰当的词语。Choose the appropriate words according to the text.

起爆时，首先把母线_____在发爆器的接线端。然后把_____插入发爆器，并转动至充电位置。当充电完成后，按下_____，发出爆破_____，提醒周围人们注意。

A. 准确连接　　　B. 钥匙　　　C. 报警按钮　　　D. 警报

语法 Grammar

朗读下面的句子。Read aloud the following sentences.

1 把钥匙转动至充电位置。

2 开采设备要运输至井下。

3 把钥匙转回至放电位置。

4 开采设备要运回仓库。

课文理解 Text Comprehension

根据课文内容，判断对错。Tell True (T) or False (F) according to the text.

把母线准确接在发爆器的接线端。	A. 是　　B. 不是
钥匙插入发爆器后，转至充电位置。	A. 是　　B. 不是
充电完成后发出爆破警报，提醒周围注意安全。	A. 是　　B. 不是
等待5秒后，转钥匙至放电位置，通电起爆。	A. 是　　B. 不是

第 25 课 Lesson 25

Qǐdòng júbù tōngfēngjī
启动局部通风机
Start the Local Ventilating Fan

复习 Revision

连线。Match.

充电　　　　　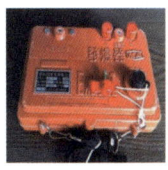　　　　　detonator

发爆器　　　　　　　　　charge

转回　　　　　　　　　　alarm

报警　　　　　　　　　　turn back

钥匙　　　　　　　　　　key

221

 ## 热身 Warm-up

下列图片你认识多少？ How many of the following pictures do you know?

júbù tōngfēngjī
局部通风机
local ventilating fan

fēngtǒng
风筒
air duct

jiētóu
接头
connector

ànniǔ
按钮
button

wǎngzhào
网罩
cover

jìnfēngkǒu
进风口
air inlet

 ## 学习生词 Words and Expressions 🎧 25-01

1	启动	qǐdòng	v.	start
2	局部	júbù	n.	local
3	通风机	tōngfēngjī	n.	ventilating fan
4	清理	qīnglǐ	v.	clean up
5	进风口	jìnfēngkǒu	n.	air inlet
6	杂物	záwù	n.	debris

第25课 | 启动局部通风机

7	网罩	wǎngzhào	*n.*	mesh cover
8	牢固	láogù	*adj.*	firm
9	高	gāo	*adj.*	tall
10	于	yú	*prep.*	(*used in comparison*) than
11	风筒	fēngtǒng	*n.*	air duct
12	正确	zhèngquè	*adj.*	correct
13	按压	ànyā	*v.*	press

词语练习 Word Exercises

1. 看图片，将相应的字母填在括号里。**Look at the pictures and fill in the corresponding letters in the brackets.**

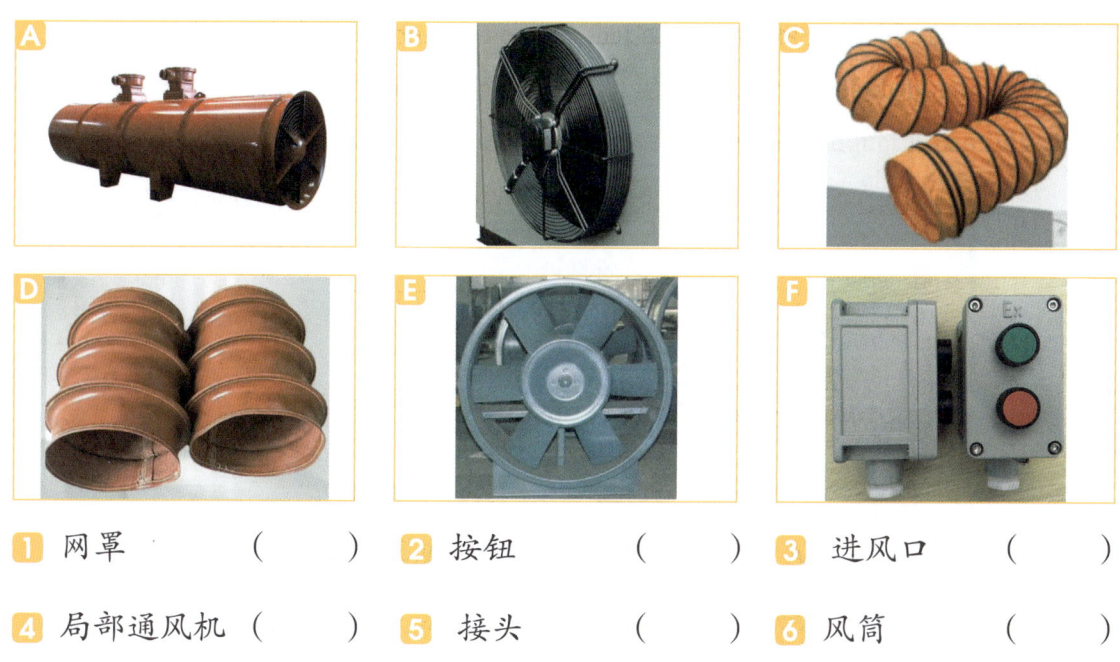

1 网罩　　（　　）　　2 按钮　　（　　）　　3 进风口　　（　　）

4 局部通风机（　　）　　5 接头　　（　　）　　6 风筒　　（　　）

2. 朗读词语搭配。Read aloud the word collocations.

❶ 启动	启动局部通风机	❷ 安装	安装安全网罩
	启动按钮	❸ 检查	检查瓦斯浓度
❹ 清理	清理煤炭	❺ 连接	连接风筒
	清理通风机	❻ 按压	按压按钮

学习课文 Text 🎧 25-02

Qǐdòng júbù tōngfēngjī
启动局部通风机

Qǐdòng júbù tōngfēngjī qián, shǒuxiān yào qīnglǐ jìnfēngkǒu qián
启动局部通风机前，首先要清理进风口前
de méitàn děng záwù, jiǎnchá ānquán wǎngzhào ānzhuāng shìfǒu láogù,
的煤炭等杂物，检查安全网罩安装是否牢固，
zài jiǎnchá jìnfēngkǒu chù wǎsī nóngdù, wǎsī nóngdù bùdé gāo yú
再检查进风口处瓦斯浓度，瓦斯浓度不得高于
0.5%, ránhòu yào jiǎnchá fēngtǒng de liánjiē shìfǒu láogù, fēngtǒng
0.5%，然后要检查风筒的连接是否牢固，风筒
jiētóu shìfǒu zhèngquè, zuìhòu ànyā qǐdòng ànniǔ.
接头是否正确，最后按压启动按钮。

Start the Local Ventilating Fan

When starting the local ventilating fan, first clean up coal and other debris in front of the air inlet, check whether the safety mesh cover is

第25课 | 启动局部通风机

installed firmly. Then check the gas concentration at the air inlet, which should not be greater than 0.5%. Afterwards, check whether the air duct is connected firmly and whether the air duct joint is correct, and finally press the start button.

课文练习 Text Exercises

1. 根据课文内容，判断对错。 Tell True (T) or False (F) according to the text.

Statements	Answer
❶ 启动局部通风机前，不用清理进风口前的杂物。	A. 是　　B. 不是
❷ 不检查安全网罩，可以启动局部通风机。	A. 是　　B. 不是
❸ 启动局部通风机时，不用检查风筒的连接。	A. 是　　B. 不是
❹ 启动局部通风机前，需要检查进风口处瓦斯浓度。	A. 是　　B. 不是

2. 根据课文内容，选词填空。 Choose the words to fill in the blanks according to the text.

❶ 启动局部通风机前，要清理进风口前的_____等_____。

　A. 杂物　　　　　　　B. 煤炭

❷ 启动局部通风机前，要检查安全网罩_____是否_____。

　A. 牢固　　　　　　　B. 安装

❸ 瓦斯浓度_____0.5%，不能_____局部通风机。

　A. 启动　　　　　　　B. 高于

❹ 按压_____按钮前，还需检查风筒的_____。

　A. 联接　　　　　　　B. 启动

学习语法 Grammar

语法点 1 Grammar Point 1

介词：于   The preposition: 于

用在形容词后表示比较。
It is used after an adjective to indicate comparison.

1. 瓦斯浓度不得高于 0.5%。The gas concentration should not be greater than 0.5%.
2. 设备的高度必须小于 5 米。The height of the equipment must be lower than 5 meters.

语法点 1 练习 Grammar Point Exercises 1

选词填空。Choose the words to fill in the blanks.

A. 于   B. 在

1. 我们的设备都_____仓库。
2. 门的高度不能低_____2 米。
3. 二氧化碳的浓度不得高_____0.1%。
4. 这条巷道的长度保持_____800 到 1000 米。

语法点 2 Grammar Point 2

小数和百分数的读法 How to read decimals and percentages

小数的表示方式是"……点……"，在个位数后面加"点"。百分数的表示方式是"百分之……"。

A decimal is shown as "…… 点 ……", with "点" used after the ones place. A percentage is shown as "百分之 ……".

---

1. Wǎsī nóngdù yīnggāi dī yú 0.5% (bǎi fēn zhī líng diǎn wǔ).
   瓦斯浓度 应该 低于 0.5%（百分之零点五）。The gas concentration should be lower than 0.5% (zero point five percent).

2. Qǔdé hégézhèng de gōngrén yǒu 92.6% (bǎi fēn zhī jiǔshí'èr diǎn liù).
   取得合格证的 工人 有92.6%（百分之九十二点六）。92.6% (ninety two point six percent) of the employees obtained the certificates.

3. Tōngguò kǎoshì de xuéshēng yǒu 90.8% (bǎi fēn zhī jiǔshí diǎn bā).
   通过 考试的 学生 有90.8%（百分之九十点八）。90.8% (ninety point eight percent) of the students passed the exam.

语法点 2 练习 Grammar Point Exercises 2

朗读下面的数字。Read aloud the following numbers.

1. 35.8%：_____

2. 42.09%：_____

3. 80.27%：_____

4. 90.01%：_____

 汉字书写 Writing Chinese Characters

 文化拓展 Culture Insight

Spring Festival

Spring Festival is also known as Chinese New Year. With a long history, it originated from the primitive beliefs and natural worship of early humans, and evolved from praying for the beginning of the year and offering sacrifices in ancient times.

As the New Year is the most important of all the festivals, and spring comes first in four seasons, Spring Festival is considered the most important traditional Chinese festival influenced by Chinese culture, some countries and regions around the world also celebrate Spring Festival.

第 25 课 | 启动局部通风机

小结 Summary

词语 Words

连线。Match.

进风口　　网罩　　通风机　　风筒　　接头　　清理

joint　　clean up　　air duct　　mesh cover　　air inlet　　ventilating fan

语法 Grammar

朗读下面的句子。Read aloud the following sentences.

1. 瓦斯浓度不得高于 0.5%。

2. 设备的高度必须小于 5 米。

3. 瓦斯浓度应该低于 0.5%（百分之零点五）。

4. 取得合格证的职工有 92.6%（百分之九十二点六）。

课文理解 Text Comprehension

根据课文内容，选词填空。Choose the words to fill in the blanks according to the text.

　　启动局部_____前，首先要_____进风口前的煤炭等杂物，检查安全网罩安装是否牢固，再_____进风口处瓦斯_____，瓦斯浓度不得高于 0.5%，然后要检查风筒的_____是否牢固，_____接头是否正确，最后_____启动按钮。

A. 清理　B. 通风机　C. 风筒　D. 联接　E. 检查　F. 按压　H. 浓度

第 26 课 Lesson 26

Ānzhuāng máogǎn
安装锚杆
Install the Anchor Rod

 复习 Revision

连线。Match.

进风口		button
按钮		mesh cover
风筒		air duct
接头		air inlet
网罩		connector
通风机		ventilating fan

第26课 | 安装锚杆

 热身 Warm-up

下列图片你认识多少？ How many of the following pictures do you know?

shùzhī
树脂
resin

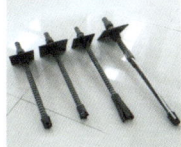
máogǎn
锚杆
anchor rod

luómào
螺帽
nut

máopán
锚盘
anchor plate

fēngdòng bānshou
风动 扳手
pneumatic wrench

shíjiān
时间
time

 学习生词 Words and Expressions 🎧 26-01

1	锚杆	máogǎn	n.	anchor rod
2	树脂药卷	shùzhī yàojuǎn	phr.	resin explosive cartridge
3	套	tào	v./n.	put on; sleeve, case
4	风动扳手	fēngdòng bānshou	phr.	pneumatic wrench
5	一边……一边……	yìbiān……yìbiān……		indicating doing two things at the same time
6	搅拌	jiǎobàn	v.	stir

231

7	时间	shíjiān	n.	time
8	为	wéi	v.	be
9	外口	wàikǒu	n.	outer opening
10	找平	zhǎopíng	v.	make level
11	锚盘	máopán	n.	anchor plate
12	拧紧	nǐngjǐn	phr.	tighten
13	螺帽	luómào	n.	nut
14	等	děng	v.	wait
15	凝固	nínggù	v.	solidify
16	抽样	chōu//yàng	v.	do a spot check
17	锚固力	máogùlì	n.	anchoring force

词语练习 Word Exercises

1. 看图片，将相应的字母填在括号里。 Look at the pictures and fill in the corresponding letters in the brackets.

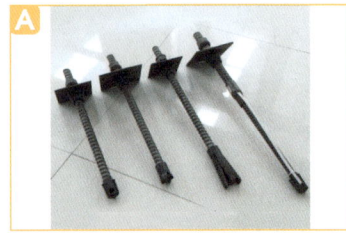

第26课 | 安装锚杆

1. 风动扳手　（　）　2. 时间　　（　）　3. 树脂药卷　（　）
4. 树脂　　　（　）　5. 连接套　（　）　6. 螺帽　　　（　）
7. 搅拌　　　（　）　8. 锚盘　　（　）　9. 锚杆　　　（　）

2. 朗读词语搭配。Read aloud the word collocations.

1. 安装	安装锚杆	2. 套上	套上锚盘
3. 树脂药卷	搅拌树脂药卷	4. 拧紧	拧紧螺帽
5. 风动扳手	装上风动扳手	6. 到	到凝固时间
	拆下风动扳手	7. 检查	检查锚固力

 学习课文　Text　26-02

Ānzhuāng máogǎn
安装 锚杆

Yòng máogǎn bǎ shùzhī yàojuǎn fàng zhì yǎn dǐ, tàoshang liánjiētào,
用 锚杆把树脂药卷放至眼底，套上 连接套，

zhuāngshang fēngdòng bānshou, yìbiān jiǎobàn yìbiān tuījìn, zhídào
装上 风动扳手，一边搅拌一边推进，直到

yǎn dǐ, jiǎobàn shíjiān wéi 30 miǎo. Chāixia fēngdòng bānshou, bǎ
眼底，搅拌时间为 30 秒。拆下风动扳手，把

máogǎnyǎn wàikǒu zhǎopíng, 15 fēnzhōng hòu, tàoshang máopán, nǐngjǐn
锚杆眼外口找平，15 分钟后，套上 锚盘，拧紧

螺帽。锚杆安装后，等树脂药卷到凝固时间，再抽样检查锚固力。

Install the Anchor Rod

Use an anchor rod to place the resin explosive cartridge to the bottom of the anchor rod opening, put on a connecting sleeve, install a pneumatic wrench, and stir while pushing until it reaches the bottom of the anchor rod opening. Stir for 30 seconds. Remove the pneumatic wrench, level the outer opening of the anchor rod opening, put on the anchor plate in 15 minutes and tighten the nut. After installing the anchor rod, perform the spot check for the anchoring force after the resin explosive cartridge solidifies.

课文练习 Text Exercises

1. 根据课文内容，判断对错。Tell True (T) or False (F) according to the text.

Statements	Answer
① 安装锚杆时，树脂药卷要放至眼底。	A. 是　　B. 不是
② 树脂药卷搅拌时间为 30 秒。	A. 是　　B. 不是
③ 拆下风动扳手，不用把锚杆眼外口找平。	A. 是　　B. 不是
④ 树脂药卷不用凝固，就可以检查锚固力。	A. 是　　B. 不是

2. 根据课文内容，选词填空。Choose the words to fill in the blanks according to the text.

① 用_____把_____放至眼底。

   A. 树脂药卷　　　　　　B. 锚杆

第26课 | 安装锚杆

2 _____ 连接套，_____ 风动扳手。

　　A. 套上　　　　　　B. 装上

3 _____ 风动扳手，_____ 螺帽。

　　A. 拧紧　　　　　　B. 拆下

4 锚杆安装后，树脂药卷到 _____ 时间，再 _____ 锚固力。

　　A. 检查　　　　　　B. 凝固

学习语法 Grammar

语法点1 Grammar Point 1

一边……一边……

用于表示两个动作同时进行。

It is used to indicate that two actions are performed simultaneously.

1 Yìbiān jiǎobàn yìbiān tuījìn.
一边 搅拌 一边 推进。Stir while pushing it.

2 Yìbiān tàoshang yìbiān nǐngjǐn.
一边 套上 一边 拧紧。Put it on while tightening it.

3 Yìbiān ānzhuāng yìbiān jiǎnchá.
一边 安装 一边 检查。Install it while checking it.

语法点1练习 Grammar Point Exercises 1

连词成句。Rearrange the words to form sentences.

1 ①你们　②一边　③一边　④推进　⑤搅拌　⑥要

2 ①工人　②安装　③检查　④锚杆　⑤一边　⑥一边

---

3 ①观察　②一边　③一边　④他们　⑤数据　⑥记录

---

4 ①工人　②拧紧　③安装　④螺帽　⑤一边　⑥一边

语法点 2　Grammar Point 2

等……，再……
表示一个动作发生在另一个动作结束之后。
It indicates that one action happens after another action.

1 Děng shùzhī yàojuǎn dào nínggù shíjiān, zài chōuyàng jiǎnchá máogùlì.
等 树脂 药卷 到 凝固 时间，再 抽样 检查 锚固力。Perform the spot check for the anchoring force after the resin explosive cartridge solidifies.

2 Děng fēngbiǎo kōngzhuàn 30 miǎo hòu, zài dǎkāi fēngbiǎo hé miǎobiǎo kāiguān.
等 风表 空转 30 秒后，再打开 风表 和 秒表 开关。Turn on the switches of the anemometer and of the stopwatch after the anemometer idles for 30 seconds.

3 Děng tiáozhěng hǎo jiǎodù, zài yòng shǒuzhǐ mànmàn yāxia ànniǔ.
等 调整 好 角度，再 用 手指 慢慢 压下 按钮。Slowly press the button with fingers after adjusting the angle.

语法点 2 练习　Grammar Point Exercises 2

连线。Match.

1 等树脂药卷到搅拌时间　　　　　再套上锚盘

2 等树脂药卷到凝固时间　　　　　再通电起爆

3 等 15 分钟以后　　　　　　　　再拆下风动扳手

4 等发出爆破警报后　　　　　　　再抽样检查锚固力

第26课 | 安装锚杆

 汉字书写 Writing Chinese Characters

 职业拓展 Career Insight

Anchor Rod

Anchor rod is the most basic component of tunnel support in contemporary coal mines. It reinforces the surrounding rock of the tunnel, allowing the surrounding rock to support itself. Anchor rod can be used in both mines and engineering technologies to reinforce the main bodies of slopes, tunnels, and dams. As a tensile component that penetrates deep into the stratum, the anchor rod is connected to the engineering structure at one end and penetrates deep into the stratum at the other end. The whole anchor rod is divided into a free section and an anchoring section. The free section refers to the area where the tension at the anchor head is transmitted to the anchor body, which aims to apply pre-stress to the anchor rod.

小结 Summary

词语 Words

连线。Match.

抽样　　风动扳手　　拧紧　　搅拌　　螺帽　　锚杆

stir　　anchor rod　　nut　　tighten　　pneumatic wrench　　do a spot check

语法 Grammar

朗读下面的句子。Read aloud the following sentences.

1. 一边搅拌一边推进。
2. 一边套上一边拧紧。
3. 等树脂药卷到凝固时间，再抽样检查锚固力。
4. 等风表空转 30 秒后，再打开风表和秒表开关。

课文理解 Text Comprehension

根据课文内容，选词填空。Choose the words to fill in the blanks according to the text.

　　用锚杆把_____放至眼底，套上连接套，装上风动扳手，一边_____一边推进，直到眼底，搅拌时间为 30 秒。_____风动扳手，把_____眼外口找平，15 分钟后，套上锚盘，_____螺帽。_____安装后，等树脂药卷到_____时间，再抽样检查_____。

　　A. 树脂药卷　B. 拆下　C. 锚杆　D. 搅拌　E. 拧紧　F. 锚固力　H. 凝固

第 27 课 Lesson 27

Jiǎnchá pídài yùnshūjī
检查皮带运输机
Check the Belt Conveyor

复习 Revision

连线。Match.

螺帽		pneumatic wrench
锚盘	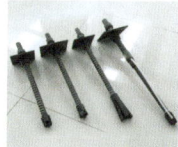	resin explosive cartridge
风动扳手		nut
树脂药卷		anchor rod
锚杆		anchor plate

 ## 热身 Warm-up

下列图片你认识多少？How many of the following pictures do you know?

jiǎnsùjī
减速机
reducer

pídài yùnshūjī
皮带运输机
belt conveyor

gǔntǒng
滚筒
rotary drum

zhóuchéng
轴承
bearing

diàndòngjī
电动机
electric motor

tuōgǔn
托辊
roller

 ## 学习生词 Words and Expressions 🎧 27-01

1	皮带运输机	pídài yùnshūjī	phr.	belt conveyor
2	电动机	diàndòngjī	n.	electric motor
3	减速机	jiǎnsùjī	n.	reducer
4	异响	yìxiǎng	n.	abnormal sound
5	滚筒	gǔntǒng	n.	rotary drum
6	温度	wēndù	n.	temperature

第27课 | 检查皮带运输机

7	合适	héshì	*adj.*	appropriate
8	均匀	jūnyún	*adj.*	even, well-distributed
9	挡	dǎng	*v.*	side, block
10	跑偏	pǎo//piān	*v.*	deviate
11	现象	xiànxiàng	*n.*	phenomenon
12	托辊	tuōgǔn	*n.*	roller
13	轴承	zhóuchéng	*n.*	bearing
14	缺油	quē yóu	*phr.*	lack oil
15	的话	dehuà	*part.*	if...
16	补充	bǔchōng	*v.*	add

词语练习 Word Exercises

1. 看图片，将相应的字母填在括号里。Look at the pictures and fill in the corresponding letters in the brackets.

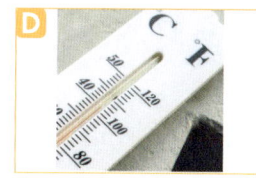

1 托辊　（　）　2 轴承　（　）　3 电动机　（　）

4 滚筒　（　）　5 减速机　（　）　6 温度　（　）

2. 朗读词语搭配。Read aloud the word collocations.

❶ 检查	检查电动机	❷ 煤炭	煤炭均匀
	检查减速机	❹ 皮带	皮带破损
❸ 温度	温度合适		皮带跑偏

 学习课文 Text 🎧 27-02

检查皮带运输机
Jiǎnchá pídài yùnshūjī

检查皮带运输机步骤：
Jiǎnchá pídài yùnshūjī bùzhòu:

1. 检查电动机、减速机有无异响，滚筒工作是否正常。
Jiǎnchá diàndòngjī、jiǎnsùjī yǒu wú yìxiǎng, gǔntǒng gōngzuò shìfǒu zhèngcháng.

2. 还要检查电动机温度是否合适。
Hái yào jiǎnchá diàndòngjī wēndù shìfǒu héshì.

3. 检查皮带上的煤炭是否均匀。
Jiǎnchá pídài shang de méitàn shìfǒu jūnyún.

4. 检查挡皮带有无破损、跑偏等现象。
Jiǎnchá dǎngpídài yǒu wú pòsǔn、pǎopiān děng xiànxiàng.

5. 检查皮带托辊轴承是否缺油，缺油的话，要及时补充。
Jiǎnchá pídài tuōgǔn zhóuchéng shìfǒu quē yóu, quē yóu dehuà, yào jíshí bǔchōng.

第27课 | 检查皮带运输机

Check the Belt Conveyor

Steps of checking the belt conveyor:

1. Check whether there is any abnormal sound from the electric motor and reducer, and whether the rotary drum is working normally.
2. In addition, check whether the motor temperature is appropriate.
3. Check whether the coal on the belt is evenly distributed.
4. Check whether there is any damage, deviation or other phenomena with the siding belt.
4. Check whether the bearing of the belt roller lacks oil. If it does, add oil in time.

课文练习 Text Exercises

1. 根据课文内容，判断对错。Tell True (T) or False (F) according to the text.

Statements	Answer
❶ 电动机、减速机有异响，皮带运输机可以正常工作。	A. 是　　B. 不是
❷ 检查皮带运输机，需要检查电动机温度。	A. 是　　B. 不是
❸ 挡皮带有破损、跑偏现象，皮带运输机没问题。	A. 是　　B. 不是
❹ 皮带托辊轴承缺油，不用及时补充。	A. 是　　B. 不是

2. 根据课文内容，选词填空。Choose the words to fill in the blanks according to the text.

❶ _____ 电动机、减速机有无 _____。　　A. 异响　　B. 检查

243

❷ 检查电动机_____是否_____。　　A. 温度　　B. 正常

❸ 检查_____有无_____、跑偏等现象。　　A. 破损　　B. 挡皮带

❹ 皮带托辊轴承_____，及时_____。　　A. 补充　　B. 缺油

学习语法 Grammar

语法点1 Grammar Point 1

副词：还　The adverb: 还

用在动词前，表示在某个范围之外有所补充。
It is used before a verb to indicate that there is an addition beyond a certain scope.

❶ 要检查电动机有无异响，还要检查温度是否正常。
Yào jiǎnchá diàndòngjī yǒu wú yìxiǎng, hái yào jiǎnchá wēndù shìfǒu zhèngcháng.
Check whether there is any abnormal sound from the electric motor, and whether the temperature is normal.

❷ 工人们要参加安全培训，还要通过考试。
Gōngrénmen yào cānjiā ānquán péixùn, hái yào tōngguò kǎoshì.
Workers need to participate in safety training, and they also need to pass the exam.

❸ 下井前要穿好工作服，还要带好矿灯和自救器等。
Xià jǐng qián yào chuānhǎo gōngzuòfú, hái yào dàihǎo kuàngdēng hé zìjiùqì děng.
Wear the work clothes with the miner's lamp and the self-rescuer before the downhole work.

语法点1练习 Grammar Point Exercises 1

把"还"放在合适的位置。Put "还" in the appropriate positions.

❶ 我 A 有 B 一个 C 操作煤电钻的 D 问题。

❷ 我们 A 今天 B 要 C 准备 D 下井。

3 A 测风 B 用皮尺、C 瓦检仪，D 有秒表和记录本。

4 努力 A 工作的 B 同时，他 C 必须好好 D 学习。

语法点 2 Grammar Point 2

> ……的话，（就）……
>
> 表示假设关系。第一个分句表示假设的前提，第二个分句表示能够得到的结果。
> It indicates a hypothetical relationship. The first clause indicates the premise of the hypothesis, and the second clause indicates the result.

1 轴承缺油的话，要及时补充。 Zhóuchéng quē yóu dehuà, yào jíshí bǔchōng. If the bearing lacks oil, add oil in time.

2 挡皮带破损的话，要进行更换。 Dǎngpídài pòsǔn dehuà, yào jìnxíng gēnghuàn. If the siding belt is damaged, replace it.

3 电动机有异响的话，就切断电源。 Diàndòngjī yǒu yìxiǎng dehuà, jiù qiēduàn diànyuán. If there is an abnormal sound from the electric motor, cut off the power supply.

语法点 2 练习 Grammar Point Exercises 2

连线。Match.

1 矿灯破损的话   要进行调整

2 皮带上煤炭不均匀的话   就表明气路通畅

3 捏扁的吸气球能恢复的话   就不能确保操作安全

4 不认真执行的话   要及时更换

 汉字书写 Writing Chinese Characters

 文化拓展 Culture Insight

Qinghai-Xizang Railway

Qinghai-Xizang Railway, also Qingzang Railway for short, is a Class I national railway connecting Xining, Qinghai Province, to Lhasa, Xizang Autonomous Region. It is one of the four major projects in the new century in China, the first railway to the hinterland of Xizang, and also the plateau railway with the highest altitude and the longest line across the world. The completion and operation of Qinghai-Xizang Railway have shortened the land transportation duration for trade between major cities in China and Nepal from 12-18 days to less than a week, promoting the development of Nepal's underdeveloped northern mountainous areas and helping Nepal to stand independently on the world political stage. At the same time, Qinghai-Xizang Railway has strengthened the ties of Xizang with other areas in China, promoted the cultural exchange between the Tibetan people and other ethnic groups, and fostered national unity.

小结 Summary

词语 Words

连线。Match.

电动机	electric motor
减速机	reducer
滚筒	rotary drum
均匀	temperature
轴承	even, well-distributed
温度	bearing

语法 Grammar

朗读下面的句子。Read aloud the following sentences.

1. 要检查电动机有无异响，还要检查温度是否正常。
2. 下井前要穿好工作服，还要带好矿灯和自救器等。
3. 轴承缺油的话，要及时补充。
4. 皮带破损的话，要进行更换。

课文理解 Text Comprehension

根据课文内容，选词填空。Choose the words to fill in the blanks according to the text.

检查皮带运输机步骤：

1. 检查_____、减速机有无_____，滚筒工作是否_____。
2. 还要检查电动机温度是否_____。
3. 检查_____上的_____是否均匀。
4. 检查挡皮带有无_____、跑偏等现象。
5. 检查皮带托辊轴承是否缺油，缺油的话，要及时_____。

A. 破损　B. 合适　C. 正常　D. 皮带　E. 异响　F. 煤炭　G. 补充　H. 电动机

第 28 课 Lesson 28

Jiǎnchá juéjìnjī
检查掘进机
Check the Tunneling Machine

复习 Revision

连线。Match.

jiǎnsùjī 减速机		rotary drum
gǔntǒng 滚筒		reducer
zhóuchéng 轴承		belt conveyor
pídài yùnshūjī 皮带运输机		bearing
diàndòngjī 电动机		roller
tuōgǔn 托辊		electric motor

职通中文 煤矿开采技术（初级篇）

 ## 热身 Warm-up

下列图片你认识多少？ How many of the following pictures do you know?

shǒubǐng
手柄
handle

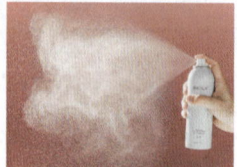
pēn wù
喷 雾
spray

jǐnglíng
警铃
alarm bell

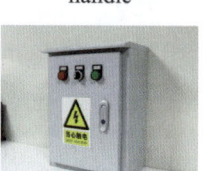
diànkòngxiāng
电控箱
electrical control box

lòu yóu
漏 油
oil leakage

 ## 学习生词 Words and Expressions 🎧 28-01

1	掘进机	juéjìnjī	n.	tunneling machine
2	开机	kāi//jī	phr.	start (a machine)
3	下列	xiàliè	adj.	following
4	均	jūn	adv.	all
5	处	chǔ	v.	(be) in
6	零位	língwèi	n.	zero position
7	内外	nèiwài	n.	internal and external
8	喷雾	pēn wù	phr.	spray

9	装置	zhuāngzhì	n.	device
10	警铃	jǐnglíng	n.	alarm bell
11	信号	xìnhào	n.	signal
12	完好	wánhǎo	adj.	intact
13	电控箱	diànkòngxiāng	n.	electrical control box
14	及	jí	conj.	and
15	照明灯	zhàomíngdēng	n.	light
16	供电	gōng diàn	phr.	power supply
17	照明	zhàomíng	v.	lighting
18	液压	yèyā	n.	hydraulic pressure
19	系统	xìtǒng	n.	system
20	油管	yóuguǎn	n.	oil pipe
21	漏油	lòu yóu	phr.	oil leakage

词语练习 Word Exercises

1. 看图片，将相应的字母填在括号里。Look at the pictures and fill in the corresponding letters in the brackets.

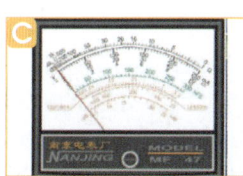

1 警铃（   ）　2 油管（   ）　3 零位（   ）　4 供电（   ）

5 手柄（   ）　6 喷雾（   ）　7 照明（   ）　8 操作（   ）

2. 选词填空。Choose the words to fill in the blanks.

1 掘进机开机前要（　　）。
   A. 检查　　B. 维修　　C. 操作

2 检查喷雾装置、警铃、（　　）等。
   A. 运行　　B. 信号　　C. 移动

3 确保照明等（　　）。
   A. 年龄　　B. 大小　　C. 可靠

4 检查液压油管无（　　）。
   A. 漏油　　B. 指挥　　C. 时间

学习课文　Text　🎧 28-02

检查掘进机
Jiǎnchá juéjìnjī

Juéjìnjī kāijī qián àn xiàliè bùzhòu jìnxíng jiǎnchá:
掘进机开机前按下列步骤进行检查：

　　　Jiǎnchá cāozuò shǒubǐng, quèbǎo cāozuò shǒubǐng jūn chǔ zài líng-
1. 检查操作手柄，确保操作手柄 均处在零

第 28 课 | 检查掘进机

wèi shang.
位上。

Jiǎnchá nèiwài pēn wù zhuāngzhì、 jǐnlíng、 xìnhào, quèbǎo wán-
2. 检查内外喷雾装置、警铃、信号，确保完

hǎo、 kěkào.
好、可靠。

Jiǎnchá diànkòngxiāng jí zhàomíngdēng, quèbǎo gōng diàn、 zhàomíng
3. 检查电控箱及照明灯，确保供电、照明

kěkào.
可靠。

Jiǎnchá yèyā xìtǒng, quèbǎo gè lèi yóuguǎn wú lòu yóu.
4. 检查液压系统，确保各类油管无漏油。

Check the Tunneling Machine

Check the tunneling machine with the following steps before starting it:

1. Check the operating handles to ensure that all the operating handles are in the zero position.
2. Check the internal and external spray devices, alarm bells and signals to ensure that they are intact and reliable.
3. Check the electrical control box and light to ensure reliable power supply and lighting.
4. Check the hydraulic system to ensure that there is no oil leakage in all sorts of oil pipes.

课文练习 Text Exercises

1. 根据课文内容，判断对错。Tell True (T) or False (F) according to the text.

Statements	Answer
❶ 掘进机开机前不需要检查。	A. 是 B. 不是

❷ 掘进机开机前需要检查操作手柄。	A. 是	B. 不是
❸ 不需要检查掘进机信号良好。	A. 是	B. 不是
❹ 需要检查掘进机无漏油。	A. 是	B. 不是

2. 根据课文内容，选词填空。Choose the words to fill in the blanks according to the text.

❶ 掘进机开机前需要（　　）是否正常。
　A. 检查　　　　　B. 维修　　　　　C. 液压系统

❷ 掘进机开机前要确保手柄均在（　　）。
　A. 顶板　　　　　B. 零位上　　　　C. 浮煤

❸ （　　）的检查，是确保掘进机供电的重点。
　A. 电控箱　　　　B. 煤粉　　　　　C. 液压系统

❹ 检查（　　），确保无漏油。
　A. 作业　　　　　B. 液压系统　　　C. 开关

 学习语法 Grammar

 语法点 1 Grammar Point 1

副词：均   The adverb: 均

用在动词前，表示"都，无例外"。多用于书面语。
It is mostly used before a verb in written Chinese to indicate "all, without exception".

❶ Quèbǎo cāozuò shǒubǐng jūn chǔ zài língwèi shang.
　确保 操作 手柄 均 处 在 零位 上 。Ensure that all the operating handles are in the zero position.

      Suǒyǒu de kuàngdēng jūn yǐ tōngguò jiǎnchá.
② 所有的 矿灯 均已通过 检查。All the miner's lamps have been checked.

      Fēngbiǎo hé miǎobiǎo jūn xū guānbì.
③ 风表 和 秒表 均须关闭。Both the anemometer and stopwatch should be turned off.

语法点 1 练习 Grammar Point Exercises 1

选词填空。Choose the words to fill in the blanks.

① 职工们_____已通过考试、取得合格证。   A. 均   B. 还

② 乘坐猴车和罐笼_____不可打闹玩耍。   A. 均   B. 还

③ 我_____有一个问题。   A. 均   B. 还

④ 调整光路可以观察目镜，_____可以拧松电池盖。   A. 均   B. 还

语法点 2 Grammar Point 2

连词：及   The conjunction: 及

用于连接并列的词或短语。也可以说"以及"。多用于书面语。
It is mostly used in written Chinese to connect juxtaposed words or phrases. "以及" can also be used.

      Wǒmen yào jiǎnchá diànkòngxiāng jí zhàomíngdēng.
① 我们要 检查 电控箱 及 照明灯。We shall check the electrical control box and light.

      Yào quèbǎo pēnwù zhuāngzhì、jǐnglíng jí xìnhào wánhǎo、kěkào.
② 要 确保 喷雾 装置、警铃及信号完好、可靠。Ensure that the spray devices, alarm bells and signals are intact and reliable.

      Guānchá mùjìng jí wēidúshù shìchuāng, bìng dúchū shùjù.
③ 观察 目镜及 微读数 视窗，并读出数据。Observe the eyepiece and the micro-reading window, and read out the data.

语法点2练习 Grammar Point Exercises 2

用"及"完成句子。Complete the sentences with "及".

1. 煤矿是由_____组成的。

2. 井下行走时,不得取下_____。

3. 下井时,皮带上要系_____。

4. 巷道可以用来_____。

汉字书写 Writing Chinese Characters

shuǐ 水 水 水 水
水 水 水 水 水

dàn 旦 旦 旦 旦
旦 旦 旦 旦 旦

yǒng 永 永 永 永 永
永 永 永 永 永

dàn 但 但 但 但 但 但 但
但 但 但 但 但

职业拓展 Career Insight

Tunneling Machine

The tunneling machine is mainly composed of eight parts: the cutting mechanism, the shipping mechanism, the traveling mechanism, the hydraulic system, the electrical system, the spray derusting system, the carrier and the frame. In terms of its working mode, it's mainly composed of the traveling mechanism, the working mechanism, the shipping mechanism, and the transfer mechanism. As the traveling mechanism advances, the cutting head in the working mechanism keeps breaking rocks and transports them away. It boasts strength such as safety, efficiency, and good tunneling quality, but it has high cost, a complex structure, and high losses.

小结 Summary

 词语 Words

根据课文内容，选择恰当的词语。Choose the appropriate words according to the text.

1. 检查_____手柄，确保操作手柄均处在_____上。
2. 检查内外_____装置、警铃、信号，确保完好、可靠。
3. 检查_____及照明灯，确保供电、照明可靠。

  A. 喷雾   B. 电控箱   C. 零位   D. 操作

 语法 Grammar

朗读下面的句子。Read aloud the following sentences.

1. 确保操作手柄均处在零位上。
2. 我们要检查电控箱及照明灯。

3 风表和秒表均须关闭。

4 观察目镜及微读数视窗，并读出数据。

课文理解 Text Comprehension

根据课文内容，判断对错。 Tell True (T) or False (F) according to the text.

检查操作手柄，确保操作手柄均处在零位上。 Check the operating handles to ensure that the operating handles are in the zero position.	A. 是　　B. 不是
检查电控箱及照明灯，确保供电、照明可靠。 Check the electric control box and light to ensure reliable power supply and lighting.	A. 是　　B. 不是
检查内外喷雾装置、警铃、信号，确保完好、可靠。 Check the internal and external spray devices, alarm bells, and signals to ensure that they are intact and reliable.	A. 是　　B. 不是
检查液压系统，确保各类油管无漏油。 Check the hydraulic system to ensure that there is no oil leakage in various oil pipes.	A. 是　　B. 不是

第 29 课 Lesson 29
Qǐdòng juéjìnjī 启动掘进机
Start the Tunneling Machine

 复习 Revision

连线。Match.

警铃　　　　　　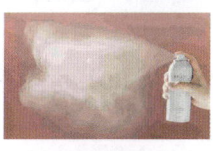　　　　　　oil leakage

漏油　　　　　　　　　　　　alarm bell

电控箱　　　　　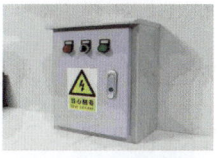　　　　　　electric control box

手柄　　　　　　　　　　　　spray

喷雾　　　　　　　　　　　　　　　　　　　handle

热身 Warm-up

下列图片你认识多少？ How many of the following pictures do you know?

zhàng'àiwù
障碍物
obstacles

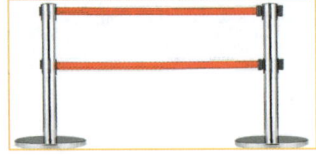
gélí
隔离
disconnect

diànlíng
电铃
electric bell

yèyābèng
液压泵
hydraulic pump

guābǎn yùnshūjī
刮板 运输机
scraper conveyor

zhuǎnzài yùnshūjī
转载 运输机
transfer conveyor

学习生词 Words and Expressions 🎧 29-01

1	一下儿	yíxiàr	q.	used after a verb to indicate one action/attempt
2	环境	huánjìng	n.	environment
3	障碍物	zhàng'àiwù	n.	obstacle
4	合上	héshang	phr.	close
5	隔离	gélí	v.	disconnect
6	接通	jiētōng	v.	turn on

7	电铃	diànlíng	n.	electric bell
8	液压泵	yèyābèng	n.	hydraulic pump
9	电机	diànjī	n.	electric machinery
10	转载运输机	zhuǎnzài yùnshūjī	phr.	transfer conveyor
11	刮板运输机	guābǎn yùnshūjī	phr.	scraper conveyor
12	截割头	jiégētóu	n.	cutting head

词语练习 Word Exercises

1. 看图片，将相应的字母填在括号里。Look at the pictures and fill in the corresponding letters in the brackets.

1 障碍物 （ ）　2 电铃 （ ）　3 隔离 （ ）

4 液压泵 （ ）　5 转载运输机（ ）　6 刮板运输机（ ）

2. 朗读词语搭配。Read aloud the word collocations.

❶ 确保	确保安全	❷ 启动	启动刮板运输机
	确保干净		启动转载运输机
❸ 接通	接通电铃	❹ 清理	清理杂物
	接通水管		清理障碍物

学习课文 Text 🎧 29-02

启动掘进机 (Qǐdòng juéjìnjī)

启动前先检查一下儿周围环境，确保周围无人和障碍物。然后按规定操作顺序启动。一般启动顺序是：首先合上隔离开关，接通电铃，发出开机信号，30秒后，启动液压泵电机，然后依次启动转载运输机、刮板运输机。最后启动截割头。

Start the Tunneling Machine

Check the surrounding environment before starting the tunneling machine to ensure that there are no people or obstacles around. Then start it following the prescribed operating sequence. Generally speaking, the starting sequence is: first turn off the disconnect switch, turn on the electric bell to send a startup signal, start the hydraulic pump motor in 30 seconds, and then start the transfer conveyor and scraper conveyor successively. Finally, start the cutting head.

课文练习 Text Exercises

1. 根据课文内容，判断对错。Tell True (T) or False (F) according to the text.

Statements	Answer
❶ 在启动掘进机前先要检查周围环境。	A. 是　　B. 不是
❷ 启动掘进机的第一步是发出开机信号。	A. 是　　B. 不是
❸ 发出开机信号30秒后才可以启动液压泵电机。	A. 是　　B. 不是
❹ 启动掘进机的最后一步是启动截割头。	A. 是　　B. 不是

2. 根据课文内容，选词填空。Choose the words to fill in the blanks according to the text.

❶ 启动掘进机前，我们要检查（　　）。
   A. 煤炭　　　　　　B. 周围环境　　　　　　C. 矿灯

❷ 接通电铃发出开机信号多少秒后可以启动液压泵电机？（　　）秒。
   A. 60　　　　　　　B. 30　　　　　　　　　C. 10

❸ 启动掘进机的第一步是（　　）。
   A. 启动转载运输机

B. 合上隔离开关

C. 接通电铃发出开机信号

4 启动掘进机的最后一步是（　　）。

A. 接通电铃发出开机信号　　B. 合上隔离开关　　C. 启动截割头

学习语法 Grammar

语法点 1 Grammar Point 1

数量词：一下儿　The quantifier: 一下儿

表示动作次数为一或动作时间短，同时也常含有轻松随意的语气。常用结构为"动词＋一下儿（＋宾语）"。

It indicates that an action occurs only once or the duration of an action is short. It also often features a relaxed and casual tone. The common structure is "verb＋一下儿（+object)".

1 　　Juéjìnjī qǐdòng qián yào xiān jiǎnchá yíxiàr zhōuwéi de huánjìng.
　　掘进机启动前要先检查一下儿周围的环境。Check the surrounding environment before starting the tunneling machine.

2 　　Qǐng nǐ shuō yíxiàr cè fēng de fāngfǎ.
　　请你说一下儿测风的方法。Please tell me the method of measuring the wind.

3 　　Nǐ dú yíxiàr kèwén.
　　你读一下儿课文。Read the text.

语法点 1 练习 Grammar Point Exercises 1

用"动词＋一下儿"填空。Fill in the blanks with "verb＋一下儿".

1 请_____你的名字。

2 请_____你的矿灯。

3 测风前先_____风表的部件是否灵活、可靠。

4 今天我们_____煤炭的形成。

语法点 2 Grammar Point 2

一般来说

表示通常的情况，常用在句首。

It is usually used at the beginning of a sentence to indicate a general situation.

1 一般来说，启动掘进机首先要合上隔离开关。Generally speaking, when starting a tunneling machine, the disconnect switch should be turned off first.

2 一般来说，水分吸收管内的硅胶颗粒若是粉红色，则需要更换。Generally speaking, if the silica gel particles inside the moisture absorption tube are pink, they need to be replaced.

3 一般来说，测风一分钟后要同时关闭风表和秒表。Generally speaking, after measuring the wind for a minute, both the anemometer and stopwatch should be turned off simultaneously.

语法点 2 练习 Grammar Point Exercises 2

完成句子。Complete the sentences.

1 一般来说，下井_____。

2 一般来说，测风_____。

3 一般来说，起爆前_____。

4 一般来说，瓦斯浓度_____。

汉字书写 Writing Chinese Characters

文化拓展 Culture Insight

Chinese Liquor

Chinese liquor has a compound flavor with esters as the main body, and koji and yeast as the saccharification starter. It uses starchy (sacchariferous) materials to brew various kinds of liquor by means of steaming, saccharification, fermentation, distillation, aging and blending. Strictly speaking, the mixed liquor blended with edible alcohol and edible spices cannot be seen as liquor. Liquor is mainly made in the upper reaches of the Yangtze River, as well as Renhuai in Guizhou, Yibin in Sichuan, and Luzhou in Sichuan in the Chishui River Basin. The latter three areas are collectively called the delta region. As the world's largest and best distilled liquor production area, its liquor industry cluster shoulders half of the Chinese liquor scene.

第29课 | 启动掘进机

小结 Summary

词语 Words

根据课文内容，选择恰当的词语。Choose the appropriate words according to the text.

　　启动前先检查一下儿周围环境，确保周围无人和障碍物。然后按规定操作顺序启动。一般启动顺序是：首先合上_____，接通_____，发出开机_____，30秒后，启动_____电机，然后依次启动转载运输机、刮板运输机。

　　A. 隔离开关　　　B. 液压泵　　　C. 电铃　　　D. 信号

语法 Grammar

朗读下面的句子。Read aloud the following sentences.

1. 掘进机启动前要先检查一下儿周围的环境。
2. 请你说一下儿测风的方法。
3. 一般来说，掘进机的启动顺序是……
4. 一般来说，测风一分钟后要同时关闭风表和秒表。

课文理解 Text Comprehension

根据课文内容，判断对错。Tell True (T) or False (F) according to the text.

在启动掘进机前先要检查周围环境。	A. 是	B. 不是
启动掘进机的第一步是发出开机信号。	A. 是	B. 不是
发出开机信号30秒后才可以启动液压泵电机。	A. 是	B. 不是
启动掘进机的最后一步是启动截割头。	A. 是	B. 不是

第 30 课 Lesson 30

关停掘进机
Guāntíng juéjìnjī
Shut down the Tunneling Machine

 复习 Revision

连线。Match.

液压泵		electric bell
电铃		hydraulic pump
隔离		obstacles
障碍物		disconnect
转载运输机		scraper conveyor
刮板运输机		transfer conveyor

第 30 课 | 关停掘进机

 热身 Warm-up

下列图片你认识多少？ How many of the following pictures do you know?

guābǎnjī
刮板机
scraper

zhǔ yóubèn
主 油 泵
main oil pump

àn
按
press

jiàshǐ
驾驶
drive

tíngzhǐ
停止
stop

jiégētóu
截割头
cutting head

 学习生词 Words and Expressions  30-01

1	退出	tuìchū	v.	remove, leave
2	驾驶	jiàshǐ	v.	drive
3	截割电机	jiégē diànjī	phr.	cutting motor
4	运转	yùnzhuǎn	v.	operate
5	铲板	chǎnbǎn	n.	shovel board
6	刮板机	guābǎnjī	n.	scraper

269

7	转载机	zhuǎnzàijī	n.	transfer machine
8	煤	méi	n.	coal
9	拉空	lākōng	phr.	be emptified
10	分别	fēnbié	adv.	respectively
11	落	luò	v.	lower, let down
12	底板	dǐbǎn	n.	bottom plate
13	打起	dǎqǐ	v.	lift
14	支撑	zhīchēng	v.	support
15	主油泵	zhǔ yóubèng	phr.	main oil pump

词语练习 Word Exercises

1. 连线。Match.

刮板机　　　　　　　　　　press

主油泵　　　　　　　　　　scraper

按　　　　　　　　　　　　drive

驾驶　　　　　　　　　　　main oil pump

第 30 课 ｜ 关停掘进机

2. 朗读词语搭配。Read aloud the word collocations.

❶	运转	运转掘进机	❷	机	刮板机
		运转采煤机			转载机
❸	退出	退出煤壁	❹	关停	关停掘进机
		退出操作位置			关停煤电站

学习课文　Text　🎧 30-02

关停掘进机
Guāntíng juéjìnjī

让截割头退出煤壁，驾驶掘进机到安全位置。按下截割电机停止按钮，截割电机停止运转。等待铲板和刮板机、转载机内的煤拉空，分别将刮板机、转载机停止按钮按下，使其停止运转。把铲板、截割头落至底板，并在打起后支撑。按下主油泵开关停止按钮，并切断电源。

271

Shut down the Tunneling Machine

Remove the cutting head from the coal wall and drive the tunneling machine to a safe position. Press the stop button of the cutting motor to stop it from operating. After the coal in the shovel board, scraper and transfer machine is emptied, press the stop buttons of the scraper and of the transfer machine respectively to stop them from operating. Lower the shovel board and cutting head to the bottom plate and lift them for support. Press the stop button on the main oil pump switch and cut off the power supply.

课文练习 Text Exercises

1. 根据课文内容，判断对错。Tell True (T) or False (F) according to the text.

Statements	Answer	
❶ 掘进机要驾驶到安全位置。	A. 是	B. 不是
❷ 按下截割电机停止按钮，截割电机停止运转了。	A. 是	B. 不是
❸ 按下刮板机停止按钮，刮板机停止运转了。	A. 是	B. 不是
❹ 按下转载机停止按钮，转载机停止运转了。	A. 是	B. 不是

2. 根据课文内容，选词填空。Choose the words to fill in the blanks according to the text.

❶ 把截割头退出_____，驾驶掘进机到_____。

    A. 安全位置   B. 煤壁

❷ 按下_____停止按钮，截割电机_____运转。

    A. 停止   B. 截割电机

3 把铲板、截割头落至_____，并在打起后_____。

A. 支撑　　　　　　　B. 底板

4 按下_____开关停止按钮，并_____电源。

A. 主油泵　　　　　　B. 切断

学习语法 Grammar

语法点 1 Grammar Point 1

副词：分别　The adverb: 分别

用在动词前，表示分头、各自行动。

It is used before a verb to indicate doing something separately.

---

1 他们分别按下刮板机、转载机的停止按钮。They press the stop buttons of the scraper and of the transfer machine respectively.
（Tāmen fēnbié ànxia guābǎnjī、zhuǎnzàijī de tíngzhǐ ànniǔ.）

2 工人们要分别向东、西开掘两条巷道。Workers need to dig two tunnels to the east and west respectively.
（Gōngrénmen yào fēnbié xiàng dōng、xī kāijué liǎng tiáo hàngdào.）

3 今天我们要分别检查瓦检仪的光路、气密性和药品。Today we're going to check the light path, airtightness and medication of the gas detector respectively.
（Jīntiān wǒmen yào fēnbié jiǎnchá wǎjiǎnyí de guānglù、qìmìxìng hé yàopǐn.）

语法点 1 练习 Grammar Point Exercises 1

用"分别"完成句子。Complete the sentences with "分别".

1 巷道的形状_____。

2 安全培训的内容_____。

3 检查瓦检仪气密性时，两手_____。

4 等铲板和刮板机、转载机内的煤拉空后，应该_____。

语法点 2 Grammar Point 2

代词：其　The pronoun: 其

表示"它"。常用结构为"其 + 动词性词语"。
It means "它". The common structure is "其 + verb / verb phrase".

1 Ànxià zhuǎnzàijī tíngzhǐ ànniǔ, shǐ qí tíngzhǐ yùnzhuǎn.
按下转载机停止按钮，使其停止运转。Press the stop button of the transfer machine to stop it from operating.

2 Jìnxíng méidiànzuàn kōngzhuàn shíyàn, quèbǎo qí yùnxíng zhèngcháng.
进行煤电钻空转实验，确保其运行正常。Conduct the idling experiment for the electric coal drill to ensure that it can operate normally.

3 Shǒu wò fēngbiǎo, shǐ qí kōngzhuàn 30 miǎo.
手握风表，使其空转 30 秒。Hold the anemometer with the hand and let it idle for 30 seconds.

语法点 2 练习 Grammar Point Exercises 2

连线。Match.

1 手握风表　　　　　　　　　　确保其能正常运行

2 按下停止按钮　　　　　　　　使其空转 30 秒

3 做煤电钻空转实验　　　　　　使其停止运转

4 调整钻头角度　　　　　　　　让其对准打眼处

 **汉字书写** Writing Chinese Characters

 **职业拓展** Career Insight

Digging Technology

Digging and backstopping are important production processes in coal mining, and fast digging of coal mine tunnels is a key technical measure to ensure high and stable production in coal mines. The level of the digging technology and the equipment is directly related to the capacity and safety of production in coal mines. Efficient mechanized digging and support technology is a necessary condition for ensuring high production and efficiency in mines, and also the development direction of tunnel digging technology.

小结 Summary

词语 Words

根据课文内容，选择恰当的词语。Choose the appropriate words according to the text.

把_____退出_____，驾驶_____到安全位置。按下截割电机停止按钮，截割电机停止_____。

A. 煤壁　　　B. 截割头　　　C. 运转　　　D. 掘进机

语法 Grammar

朗读下面的句子。Read aloud the following sentences.

1. 他们分别将刮板机、转载机停止按钮按下。
2. 工人们要分别向东、西开掘两条巷道。
3. 按下转载机的停止按钮，使其停止运转。
4. 手握风表，使其空转30秒。

课文理解 Text Comprehension

根据课文内容，选词填空。Choose the words to fill in the blanks according to the text.

1. 让截割头退出煤壁，驾驶掘进机到_____。　A. 安全位置　B. 工作面
2. 按下截割电机停止按钮，_____停止运转。　A. 安全帽　B. 截割电机
3. 把铲板、截割头落至底板，并在打起后_____。　A. 工人　B. 支撑
4. 按下主油泵开关停止按钮，并切断_____。　A. 矿灯　B. 电源

第 31 课 Lesson 31
检查采煤机 Jiǎnchá cǎiméijī
Check the Coal Mining Machine

 复习 Revision

连线。Match.

液压泵　　　　　　　　　　electric bell

电铃　　　　　　　　　　hydraulic pump

隔离　　　　　　　　　　　obstacles

障碍物　　　　　　　　　　disconnect

277

 **热身 Warm-up**

下列图片你认识多少？ How many of the following pictures do you know?

jiéchǐ
截齿
cutting pick

ànniǔ
按钮
button

wēndù
温度
temperature

kāiguān
开关
switch

lěngquè pēnwù
冷却喷雾
cooling spray

yíbiǎo xiǎnshì
仪表显示
instrument display

 **学习生词 Words and Expressions** 🎧 31-01

1	采煤机	cǎiméijī	n.	coal mining machine
2	截齿	jiéchǐ	n.	cutting pick
3	破裂	pòliè	v.	be broken
4	断裂	duànliè	v.	fracture
5	手把	shǒubà	n.	handle
6	卡住	qiǎzhù	phr.	be stuck
7	冷却喷雾	lěngquè pēnwù	phr	cooling spray
8	仪表显示	yíbiǎo xiǎnshì	phr.	instrument display

第 31 课 | 检查采煤机

9	强劲	qiángjìng	*adj.*	strong
10	且	qiě	*conj.*	and
11	参数	cānshù	*n.*	parameter

词语练习 Word Exercises

1. 看图片，将相应的字母填在括号里。Look at the pictures and fill in the corresponding letters in the brackets.

1 仪表显示　（　） 　2 截齿　（　） 　3 开关　（　）

4 手把　（　） 　5 按钮　（　） 　6 采煤机　（　）

7 温度　（　） 　8 电缆　（　） 　9 冷却喷雾　（　）

2. 朗读词语搭配。Read aloud the word collocations.

❶ 检查	检查瓦斯浓度	❷ 正常	冷却喷雾正常
	检查工作面		仪表显示正常
	检查截齿		手把正常

学习课文 Text 🎧 31-02

检查采煤机
Jiǎnchá cǎiméijī

检查采煤机电缆、截齿，确保电缆无磨损或破裂，截齿无松动或断裂。

检查采煤机手把、按钮、开关，确保手把灵活、可靠，按钮、开关无卡住或松动等情况。

检查采煤机冷却喷雾、仪表显示，确保喷雾均匀、强劲，且油压、温度等参数在正常范围内显示。

Check the Coal Mining Machine

Check the cables and cutting picks of the coal mining machine to ensure that the cables are not worn or broken, and that the cutting picks are not loose or fractured.

Check the handles, buttons, and switches of the coal mining machine to ensure that the handles are flexible and reliable, and that the buttons and switches are not stuck or loose.

Check the cooling spray and instrument display of the coal mining machine to ensure that the spraying is even and strong, and the parameters such as oil pressure and temperature are displayed within the normal range.

课文练习 Text Exercises

1. 根据课文内容，判断对错。Tell True (T) or False (F) according to the text.

Statements	Answer	
❶ 首先检查电缆、截齿的破裂或松动情况。	A. 是	B. 不是
❷ 开关、按钮、手把不需要检查。	A. 是	B. 不是
❸ 冷却喷雾不正常也可以开机。	A. 是	B. 不是
❹ 需要确保油压、温度等参数在正常范围内显示。	A. 是	B. 不是

2. 根据课文内容，选词填空。Choose the words to fill in the blanks according to the text.

❶ 确保采煤机的_____无磨损或破裂、_____无松动或断裂。

　A. 截齿　　　　　　B. 电缆

❷ 确保采煤机的手把、按钮、开关，手把灵活可靠，无卡住或_____。

　A. 开关　　　　　　B. 松动

❸ 确保采煤机的冷却_____均匀、强劲。

　A. 喷雾　　　　　　B. 仪表显示

4 确保_____、_____等仪表参数在正常范围内显示。

　　A. 油压　　　　　　B. 温度

语法点 1　Grammar Point 1

连词：且　　The conjunction: 且

用于连接并列的动词、形容词性词语或分句等。表示几个动作同时进行或几种性质同时存在。也可以说"并且"。

It is used to connect juxtaposed verbs / verb phrases, adjectives / adjective phrases, or clauses, indicating the simultaneous occurrence of several actions or the coexistence of several properties. "并且" is also used.

1 　　Jīqì diànlǎn wú mósǔn, qiě jiéchǐ wú sōngdòng huò duànliè.
　　机器电缆无磨损，且截齿无松动或断裂。The cables are not worn or broken, and the cutting picks are not loose or fractured.

2 　　Cǎiméijī lěngquè pēnwù bìxū jūnyún qiě qiángjìng.
　　采煤机冷却喷雾必须均匀且强劲。The cooling spraying of the coal mining machine must be even and strong.

3 　　Yào quèbǎo pēnwù jūnyún, qiě yóuyā、wēndù děng cānshù zhèngcháng.
　　要确保喷雾均匀，且油压、温度等参数正常。Ensure that the spraying is even and strong, and the parameters such as oil pressure and temperature are displayed within the normal range.

语法点 1 练习　Grammar Point Exercises 1

连词成句。Rearrange the words to form sentences.

1 ①钻头　②打眼处　③将　④调整好　⑤且　⑥角度　⑦对准

_____

2 ①进气　②伸入　③且　④握住　⑤检测区　⑥胶管口

_____

第31课 | 检查采煤机

3 ①风表　②方向　③且　④30秒　⑤垂直　⑥风流的　⑦空转

_____

4 ①在井下　②要　③人行道　④且　⑤走　⑥信号灯　⑦注意

_____

语法点 2 Grammar Point 2

在……（的）范围内

表示在某个界限内。在句中作状语或补语。

It is used as an adverbial or complement in a sentence to indicate within a certain range.

1. Yào quèbǎo cānshù zài zhèngcháng fànwéi nèi xiǎnshì.
要 确保 参数 在 正常 范围内显示。Ensure that the parameters are displayed within the normal range.

2. Shíyàn shùjù yīng zài 50 dào 100 de fànwéi nèi.
实验数据应在50到100的范围内。The experimental data should be within the range of 50 to 100.

3. Wǎsī nóngdù yào zài 0% dào 0.5% de fànwéi nèi.
瓦斯浓度要在0%到0.5%的范围内。The gas concentration should be within the range of 0% to 0.5%.

语法点 2 练习 Grammar Point Exercises 2

用"在……（的）范围内"完成句子。Complete the sentences with "在……（的）范围内".

1 瓦斯浓度应该_____。

2 测风时，风表空转的时间_____。

3 巷道的高度_____。

4 我们的学习时间_____。

汉字书写 Writing Chinese Characters

文化拓展 Culture Insight

Zongzi

Zongzi, a traditional Chinese food made of steamed glutinous rice wrapped in reed leaves, is often served on Dragon Boat Festival. It is one of the traditional foods with the longest history and the most profound culture in China, and has been spread to many regions. The custom of eating *zongzi* on Dragon Boat Festival has been popular not only in China, but also in other countries in East Asia.

第 31 课 | 检查采煤机

小结 Summary

词语 Words

根据课文内容，选择恰当的词语。Choose the appropriate words according to the text.

检查采煤机_____、_____，确保喷雾均匀、强劲，油压、温度等参数在_____范围内显示。

A. 仪表显示　　　B. 冷却喷雾　　　C. 正常

语法 Grammar

朗读下面的句子。Read aloud the following sentences.

1. 机器电缆无磨损，且截齿无松动或断裂。
2. 采煤机冷却喷雾必须均匀且强劲。
3. 要确保参数在正常范围内显示。
4. 瓦斯浓度要在 0 到 0.5% 的范围内。

课文理解 Text Comprehension

根据课文内容，判断对错。Tell True (T) or False (F) according to the text.

1 需要检查瓦斯浓度。	A. 是	B. 不是
2 手把、按钮、开关不用检查。	A. 是	B. 不是
3 电缆有破裂或截齿有断裂时也可以开机。	A. 是	B. 不是
4 最后检查冷却喷雾、仪表显示是否正常。	A. 是	B. 不是

第 32 课 Lesson 32
启动采煤机 Qǐdòng cǎiméijī
Start the Coal Mining Machine

 复习 Revision

连线。Match.

 　　shǒubà
　　　　　　　　手把　　　　　　cable

 　　diànlǎn
　　　　　　　　电缆　　　　　　handle

 　　lěngquè pēnwù
　　　　　　　　冷却 喷雾　　　　cutting pick

 　　cǎiméijī
　　　　　　　　采煤机　　　　　coal mining machine

 　　jiéchǐ
　　　　　　　　截齿　　　　　　cooling spray

第32课 | 启动采煤机

热身 Warm-up

下列图片你认识多少？How many of the following pictures do you know?

ànxia
按下
press

dǎkāi
打开
turn on

sǎshuǐ
洒水
sprinkle water

fámén
阀门
valve

学习生词 Words and Expressions 🎧 32-01

1	如下	rúxià	v.	be as follows
2	闭锁按钮	bìsuǒ ànniǔ	phr.	locking button
3	洒水	sǎ shuǐ	phr.	sprinkle water
4	阀门	fámén	n.	valve
5	附近	fùjìn	n.	(in the) vicinity (of)
6	即	jí	v.	be

词语练习 Word Exercises

1. 朗读词语搭配。Read aloud the word collocations.

❶ 按下	按下按钮	❷ 打开	打开阀门
	按下开关		打开喷雾洒水

2. 看图片，将对应的词语填在括号里。Look at the pictures and fill in the corresponding letters in the brackets.

1 闭锁按钮　（　　） 2 合上　　　（　　） 3 步骤　　　（　　）

4 截齿　　　（　　） 5 信号　　　（　　） 6 打开　　　（　　）

7 洒水　　　（　　） 8 阀门　　　（　　） 9 按下　　　（　　）

 学习课文　Text　 32-02

Qǐdòng　cǎiméijī
启动采煤机

Cǎiméijī qǐdòng bùzhòu rúxià:
采煤机启动步骤如下：

Dǎkāi cǎiméijī de bìsuǒ ànniǔ.
1. 打开采煤机的闭锁按钮。

第32课 | 启动采煤机

Dǎkāi cǎiméijī de sǎ shuǐ fámén, kāishǐ sǎ shuǐ.
2. 打开采煤机的洒水阀门，开始洒水。

Héshang cǎiméijī de gélí kāiguān shǒubà.
3. 合上采煤机的隔离开关手把。

Fāchū qǐdòng cǎiméijī de xìnhào, jiǎnchá bìng quèbǎo cǎiméijī gǔntǒng fùjìn wú rényuán hé zhàng'àiwù.
4. 发出启动采煤机的信号，检查并确保采煤机滚筒附近无人员和障碍物。

Ànxia qǐdòng ànniǔ, cǎiméijī jí qǐdòng wánchéng.
5. 按下启动按钮，采煤机即启动完成。

Start the Coal Mining Machine

The steps of starting the coal mining machine are as follows:

1. Turn on the locking button of the coal mining machine.
2. Turn on the sprinkler valve of the coal mining machine and start to sprinkle water.
3. Close the disconnect switch handle of the coal mining machine.
4. Send a signal of starting the coal mining machine, check and ensure that there are no people or obstacles near the rotary drum of the coal mining machine.
5. Press the start button to start the coal mining machine.

课文练习 Text Exercises

1. 根据课文内容，判断对错。Tell True (T) or False (F) according to the text.

Statements	Answer
❶ 采煤机启动前，需要先打开采煤机闭锁按钮。	A. 是　　B. 不是

❷ 采煤机的洒水阀门不需要打开。	A. 是	B. 不是
❸ 合上隔离开关手把后才能发动启动采煤机信号。	A. 是	B. 不是
❹ 最后一步是按下采煤机启动按钮。	A. 是	B. 不是

2. 根据课文内容，选词填空。Choose the words to fill in the blanks according to the text.

❶ 首先打开采煤机的闭锁_____。

　A. 开关　　　　　　B. 按钮

❷ 打开采煤机洒水阀门，开始_____。

　A. 洒水　　　　　　B. 工作

❸ 合上采煤机_____开关手把。

　A. 隔离　　　　　　B. 冷却喷雾

❹ 发出启动采煤机_____，确保滚筒附近无人员和障碍物。

　A. 信号　　　　　　B. 开关

学习语法 Grammar

语法点1 Grammar Point 1

动词：如下　The verb: 如下

表示如同下面所列举或叙述的。常用结构为"名词＋如下""动词＋如下＋名词"。
It means as listed or described below. The common structure is "noun ＋ 如下", or "verb ＋ 如下 ＋ noun".

第32课 | 启动采煤机

> ① Xià jǐngqián de zhǔnbèi gōngzuò rúxià: ......
> 下井前的准备工作如下：…… The downhole work preparations are as follows: ...
>
> ② Qǐdòng juéjìnjī yào jìnxíng rúxià cāozuò: ......
> 启动掘进机要进行如下操作：…… To start the tunneling machine, the following operations need to be performed: ...

语法点1练习 Grammar Point Exercises 1

连词成句。Rearrange the words to form sentences.

1. ①采煤机 ②如下 ③启动 ④步骤

   _____

2. ①如下 ②洒水阀门 ③所示（suǒshì, as indicated） ④采煤机

   _____

3. ①准备 ②的 ③测风前 ④如下 ⑤工作

   _____

4. ①进行 ②关停 ③如下 ④要 ⑤操作 ⑥煤电钻

   _____

语法点2 Grammar Point 2

> ……即……
>
> 用于表示某种情况实现的充分条件。含有轻松、和缓的语气。
> It is used to indicate sufficient conditions for achieving a certain situation. It features a relaxed and mild tone.

> ① Ànxia qǐdòng ànniǔ, cǎiméijī jí qǐdòng wánchéng.
> 按下启动按钮，采煤机即启动 完成。Press the start button to start the coal mining machine.
>
> ② Zuòhǎo zhǔnbèi gōngzuò jí kě xià jǐng.
> 做好 准备 工作 即可下 井。Make preparations to start the downhole work.

语法点 2 练习 Grammar Point Exercises 2

连线。Match.

① 有"禁止入内"标志　　　　　　　即发出爆破警报

② 测风一分钟后　　　　　　　　　即表明不得进入

③ 按下报警按钮　　　　　　　　　即能取得合格证

④ 通过安全考试　　　　　　　　　即可关闭风表开关

汉字书写 Writing Chinese Characters

shī 尸 尸 尸
尸 尸 尸 尸 尸

zhǐ 止 止 止 止
止 止 止 止 止

hù 户 户 户 户
户 户 户 户 户

bù 步 步 步 步 步 步
步 步 步 步 步

 职业拓展 Career Insight

Smart Mine

"Smart mine" refers to the use of artificial intelligence, industrial Internet information technology, automatic control and other modern technologies to develop and utilize coal mines, so that all the systems can be fully integrated and perceived. It includes the ability of adaptive learning to realize the full intelligent and automatic operation of the coal mine in all links of development, mining, ventilation, washing and dressing, safety assurance and transportation.

 小结 Summary

 词语 Words

朗读下面的短语。Read aloud the following phrases.

| 闭锁按钮 | 洒水阀门 | 隔离开关 |
| 发出信号 | 合上手把 | 启动采煤机 |

 语法 Grammar

朗读下面的句子。Read aloud the following sentences.

1. 采煤机启动步骤如下。
2. 下井前的准备工作如下。
3. 按下启动按钮,采煤机即启动完成。
4. 做好准备工作即可下井。

课文理解 Text Comprehension

根据课文内容，判断对错。 Tell True (T) or False (F) according to the text.

采煤机启动前，需要先打开采煤机闭锁按钮。	A. 是	B. 不是
采煤机的洒水阀门不需要打开。	A. 是	B. 不是
合上隔离开关手把后才能发动启动采煤机信号。	A. 是	B. 不是
最后一步是按下采煤机启动按钮。	A. 是	B. 不是

第 33 课 Lesson 33
Guāntíng cǎiméijī
关停采煤机
Shut down the Coal Mining Machine

 复习 Revision

连线。Match.

阀门　　　　　　　　　　sprinkle water

洒水　　　　　　　　　　press

按下　　　　　　　　　　valve

隔离开关　　　　　　　　open

打开　　　　　　　　　　disconnect switch

职通中文 煤矿开采技术（初级篇）

热身 Warm-up

下列图片你认识多少？ How many of the following pictures do you know?

pòsuì
破碎
broken

xíngzǒu
行走
walk

tíngzhǐ yùnzhuǎn
停止 运转
stop the operation

zhěngjié
整洁
clean and tidy

学习生词 Words and Expressions 🎧 33-01

1	破碎	pòsuì	v.	be broken
2	排	pái	v.	discharge
3	尽	jìn	v.	to the utmost
4	接着	jiēzhe	adv.	then
5	速度	sùdù	n.	speed
6	降	jiàng	v.	reduce
7	整洁	zhěngjié	adj.	clean and tidy

词语练习 Word Exercises

1. 朗读词语搭配。Read aloud the word collocations.

| ❶ 断开 | 断开隔离开关 | disconnect the disconnect switch |
| | 断开电缆 | disconnect the cable |

296

❷ 关闭	关闭手把	turn off the handle
	关闭洒水阀门	turn off the sprinkler valve

2. 看图片，将相应的字母填在括号里。**Look at the pictures and fill in the corresponding letters in the brackets.**

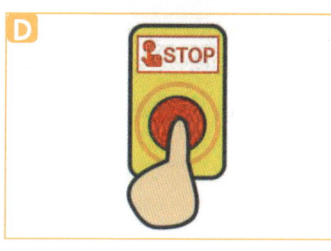

❶ 整洁　　　（　　）　❷ 操作开关　　（　　）　❸ 破碎　　　（　　）

❹ 速度　　　（　　）　❺ 停止运转　　（　　）　❻ 关停　　　（　　）

学习课文　Text　🎧 33-02

Guāntíng cǎiméijī
关停采煤机

Cǎiméijī guāntíngbùzhòu rúxià:
采煤机关停步骤如下：

1. Bǎ cǎiméijī guāntíng zài ānquán wèizhì.
   把采煤机关停在安全位置。
2. Bǎ gǔntǒng nèi de pòsuì méitàn páijìn, jiēzhe bǎ xíngzǒu sùdù jiàngdào líng.
   把滚筒内的破碎煤炭排尽,接着把行走速度降到零。
3. Ànxia cǎiméijī de tíngzhǐ ànniǔ, shǐ cǎiméijī tíngzhǐ yùnzhuǎn.
   按下采煤机的停止按钮,使采煤机停止运转。
4. Guānbì sǎ shuǐ fámén hé suǒyǒu cāozuò kāiguān.
   关闭洒水阀门和所有操作开关。
5. Qīnglǐ cǎiméijī shang de méitàn, bǎochí cǎiméijī zhěngjié.
   清理采煤机上的煤炭,保持采煤机整洁。

Shut down the Coal Mining Machine

The steps of shutting down the coal mining machine are as follows:

1. Shut down the coal mining machine in a safe position.
2. Discharge all the broken coal in the rotary drum, and then reduce the traveling speed to zero.
3. Press the stop button of the coal mining machine to stop its operation.
4. Close the sprinkler valve and turn off all the operating switches.
5. Clean up the coal on the coal mining machine and keep it clean and tidy.

课文练习 Text Exercises

1. 根据课文内容，判断对错。Tell True (T) or False (F) according to the text.

Statements	Answer	
❶ 把采煤机停在采煤工作面的安全位置。	A. 是	B. 不是
❷ 停机时需把行走速度降到零。	A. 是	B. 不是
❸ 停机时不需要关闭洒水阀门。	A. 是	B. 不是
❹ 需要保持采煤机的整洁。	A. 是	B. 不是

2. 根据课文内容，选词填空。Choose the words to fill in the blanks.

❶ 把采煤机停在采煤工作面的（　　）位置。
　　A. 安全　　　　　　B. 附近

❷ 停机时需把行走速度降到（　　）。
　　A. 运动　　　　　　B. 零

❸ 采煤机停机后，需关闭（　　）和所有操作开关。
　　A. 洒水阀门　　　　B. 隔离开关

❹ 清理采煤机上的（　　），保持采煤机整洁。
　　A. 煤炭　　　　　　B. 障碍物

学习语法 Grammar

语法点 1 Grammar Point 1

动词：尽　　The verb: 尽

用在动词后，表示无剩余。

It is used after a verb to indicate that there are no remaining items.

> Bǎ gǔntǒng nèi de pòsuì méitàn páijìn.
> ① 把 滚筒 内的 破碎煤炭排尽。Discharge all the broken coal in the rotary drum.
>
> Suǒyǒu de méitàn dōu yǐ ránjìn.
> ② 所有的煤炭 都已燃尽。All the coal has been burned out.
>
> Méitàn yào děng yòngjìn zài cǎigòu.
> ③ 煤炭要 等 用尽再采购。Coal should not be purchased until it is used up.

语法点1练习 Grammar Point Exercises 1

连词成句。Rearrange the words to form sentences.

① ①把 ②破碎 ③滚筒 ④煤炭 ⑤内 ⑥的 ⑦尽 ⑧排

_____

② ①我们 ②煤炭 ③的 ④尽 ⑤已 ⑥都 ⑦燃

_____

③ ①把 ②排 ③气体 ④吸气球 ⑤内 ⑥的 ⑦尽

_____

④ ①煤炭 ②采购 ③用 ④后 ⑤尽 ⑥再 ⑦都

_____

语法点2 Grammar Point 2

> 连词：接着　　The conjunction: 接着
>
> 表示一件事发生后，马上发生另一件事。
> It indicates that after one thing happens, another thing happens immediately.
>
> Jiēzhe bǎ xíngzǒu sùdù jiàng wéi líng.
> ① 接着把行走速度降为零。Then reduce the walking speed to zero.
>
> Jiēzhe àn guīdìng cāozuò shùnxù qǐdòng juéjìnjī.
> ② 接着按规定 操作 顺序 启动掘进机。Then start the tunneling machine according to the prescribed operating sequence.

语法点 2 练习 Grammar Point Exercises 2

用"接着"完成句子。Complete the sentences with "接着".

1. 15 分钟后，先套上锚盘，_____。
2. 把电雷管插入孔眼，_____。
3. 把瓦检仪挂在脖子上，_____。
4. 将药卷推入钻孔底部，_____。

汉字书写 Writing Chinese Characters

tīng 厅 厅 厅 厅
厅 厅 厅 厅 厅

shén 什 什 什 什
什 什 什 什 什

shēng 升 升 升 升
升 升 升 升 升

xíng 行 行 行 行 行 行
行 行 行 行 行

文化拓展 Culture Insight

Jade

Jade has been favored since ancient times. People endowed it with various beautiful symbolic meanings and gave it as a souvenir or gift to their friends and relatives to express their wishes and prayers on special anniversaries.

小结 Summary

词语 Words

根据课文内容，选择恰当的词语。Choose the appropriate words according to the text.

把采煤机_____在安全位置。按下采煤机的停止按钮，使采煤机_____。_____采煤机上的煤炭，保持采煤机_____。

A. 关停　　　B. 停止运转　　　C. 整洁　　　D. 清理

语法 Grammar

朗读下面的句子。Read aloud the following sentences.

1 把滚筒内的破碎煤炭排尽。

2 所有的煤炭都已燃尽。

3 把滚筒内的破碎煤炭排尽，接着把行走速度降到零。

4 先确保周围无人和障碍物，接着按规定操作顺序启动掘进机。

课文理解 Text Comprehension

根据课文内容，判断对错。Tell True (T) or False (F) according to the text.

把采煤机停在采煤工作面的安全位置。	A. 是	B. 不是
停机时需把行走速度降到零。	A. 是	B. 不是
停机时不需要关闭洒水阀门。	A. 是	B. 不是
需要保持采煤机整洁。	A. 是	B. 不是

第 34 课 Lesson 34
启动刮板运输机 Qǐdòng guābǎn yùnshūjī
Start the Scraper Conveyor

 复习 Revision

连线。Match.

tíngzhǐ yùnzhuǎn 停止 运转		speed
sùdù 速度		stop the operation
zhěngjié 整洁		broken
xíngzǒu 行走		clean and tidy
pòsuì 破碎		walk

 **热身 Warm-up**

下列图片你认识多少？ How many of the following pictures do you know?

sījī
司机
driver

wèizhì
位置
position

xìnhào
信号
signal

diàndòngjī
电动机
electric motor

fāngxiàng
方向
direction

ànniǔ
按钮
button

shuǐlóngtóu
水龙头
faucet

cāozuò
操作
operate

pànduàn
判断
determine

 **学习生词 Words and Expressions** 🎧 34-01

1	司机	sījī	*n.*	driver
2	其他	qítā	*pron.*	other

3	部位	bùwèi	n.	part
4	试	shì	v.	test
5	判断	pànduàn	v.	determine
6	刮板链	guābǎnliàn	n.	scraper chain
7	半	bàn	num.	half
8	周	zhōu	m.	circle
9	停机	tíng//jī	v.	shut down
10	了	le	part.	indicating the completion of an action
11	降尘	jiàngchén	v.	remove dust
12	水龙头	shuǐlóngtóu	n.	faucet

词语练习 Word Exercises

1. 看图片，将相应的字母填在括号里。Look at the pictures and fill in the corresponding letters in the brackets.

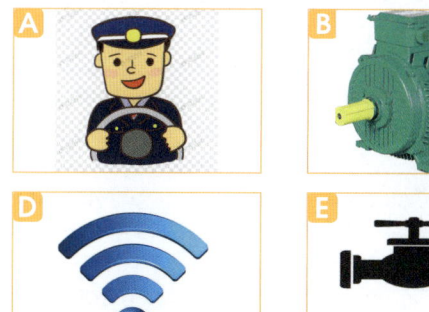

1 水龙头　　(　　)　**2** 司机　　　(　　)　**4** 按钮　　　(　　)

5 电动机　　(　　)　**3** 信号　　　(　　)　**6** 方向　　　(　　)

2. 朗读词语搭配。Read aloud the word collocations.

1	打开	打开水龙头	turn on the faucet
		打开书本	open the book
2	启动	启动电动机	start the electric motor
		启动车辆	start the vehicle
3	判断	判断方向	determine the direction
		判断对错	determine what is right and what is wrong

学习课文　Text　🎧 34-02

启动刮板运输机
Qǐdòng guābǎn yùnshūjī

在启动刮板运输机时，司机首先要发出开机信号，确保其他人员离开转动部位，然后进行试运转，判断运输机的运转方向。试运转时先按启动按钮，当刮板链运转半周后再停机。试运转正常了，按下启动按钮，启动刮板

第34课 | 启动刮板运输机

yùnshūjī, bìng dǎkāi jiàngchén shuǐlóngtóu, jìnxíng sǎ shuǐ jiàngchén.
运输机，并打开降尘水龙头，进行洒水降尘。

Start the Scraper Conveyor

When starting the scraper conveyor, the driver must first send a start signal to ensure that other personnel leave the rotating parts, and then conduct a test run to determine the operating direction of the conveyor. Press the start button first during the test run, and then shut down the scraper conveyor after the scraper chain has run for half a circle. When the test run gets normal, press the start button to start the scraper conveyor, and turn on the dust-removing faucet to sprinkle water and remove dust.

课文练习 Text Exercises

1. 根据图片提示填空。Fill in the blanks according to the pictures.

启动刮板运输机步骤为：

❶ 发出（　　）

❷ 进行试运转，判断运输机的（　　）

❸ 按下两次启动（　　）　　❹ 刮板运输机运转后，打开（　　）

2. 根据课文内容，判断对错。Tell True (T) or False (F) according to the text.

Statements	Answer	
① 司机启动刮板运输机时可以在任一位置进行操作。	A. 是	B. 不是
② 司机在开启刮板输送机前要发出开机信号。	A. 是	B. 不是
③ 在刮板运输机试车时要判断电动机的转动方向。	A. 是	B. 不是
④ 刮板运输机运转时，要打开洒水水龙头。	A. 是	B. 不是

学习语法 Grammar

语法点1 Grammar Point 1

代词：其他　The pronoun: 其他

表示"别的"。常用结构为"其他（+的）+名词"。

It indicates "other (people or things)". The common structure is "其他（+的）+ noun".

① Quèbǎo qítā rényuán líkāi zhuàndòng bùwèi.
　确保其他人员 离开 转动 部位。Ensure that other personnel leave the rotating parts.

② Hái yǒu qítā xūyào zhǔnbèi de yíqì.
　还 有其他需要准备 的仪器。There are other instruments that need to be prepared.

③ Wǒmen méiyǒu qítā de jiǎnchá fāngfǎ.
　我们 没有其他的检查 方法。We don't have other inspection methods.

语法点1练习 Grammar Point Exercises 1

连词成句。Rearrange the words to form sentences.

① ①其他　②把　③连接　④和　⑤母线　⑥脚线　⑦起来

2 ①我们　②不　③其他　④的　⑤采购　⑥设备　⑦需要

_____

3 ①巷道　②有　③形状　④还　⑤的　⑥其他

_____

4 ①没有　②要　③周围　④其他　⑤人　⑥确保

_____

语法点 2　Grammar Point 2

语气助词：了　The modal particle: 了

用于句末，表示情况的变化或新情况的出现。
It is used at the end of a sentence to indicate a change in situation or the emergence of a new situation.

1 试 运转 正常 了。　Shì yùnzhuǎn zhèngcháng le.　The test run is normal.

2 煤电钻 关停 了。　Méidiànzuàn guāntíng le.　The electric coal drill has been shut down.

3 测 风 前 的 准备 工作 做好 了。　Cè fēng qián de zhǔnbèi gōngzuò zuòhǎo le.　Preparations for measuring the wind are done.

语法点 2 练习　Grammar Point Exercises 2

用"了"完成句子。Complete the sentences with "了".

1 _____，现在可以下井。

2 _____，现在可以打开风表和秒表开关。

3 _____，表明瓦检仪气路通畅。

4 _____，可以抽样检查锚固力。

汉字书写 Writing Chinese Characters

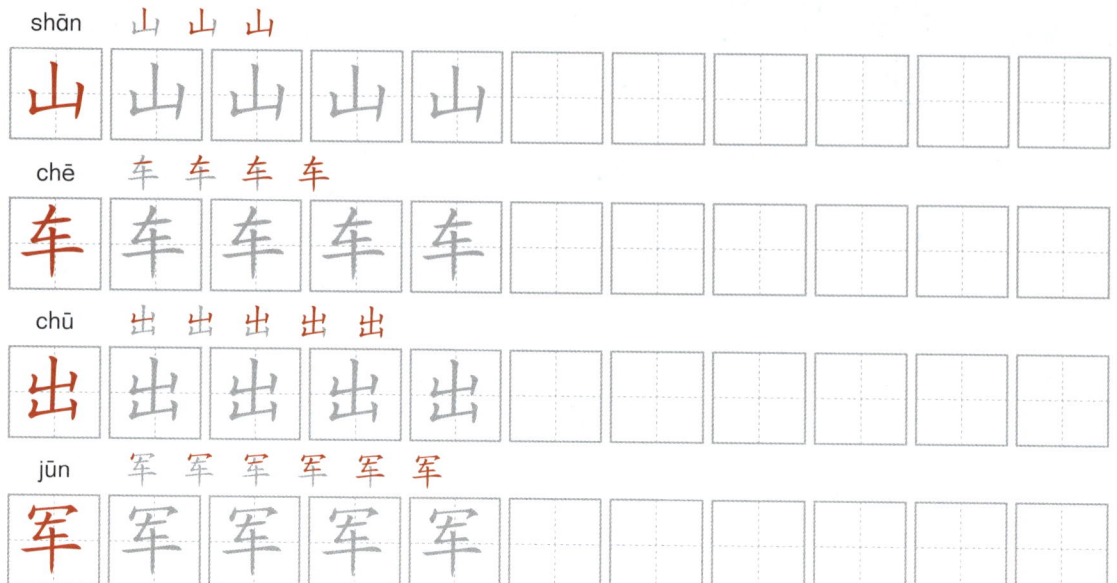

文化拓展 Culture Insight

China High-Speed Railway

    The construction of high-speed railway symbolizes China's ongoing new industrial revolution. China's unique culture, the diligence and innovation of Chinese people have enabled its high-speed railway technology (as a world's leader) to be available in a short period. China high-speed railway is seeing a new era of intelligent high-speed railway development, where new technologies such as cloud computing, big data, the Internet, mobile Internet, artificial intelligence, and Beidou navigation are widely used to make available the comprehensive perception, extensive interconnection, integrated processing, active learning, and scientific decision-making of high-speed railway mobile equipment, infrastructure, and information between internal and external environments.

As of 2019, the highest operating speed of high-speed railway trains in China was 350 km/h, ranking first worldwide. As of January 13, 2023, the operating mileage of railways in China soared from 98,000 km in 2012 to 155,000 km in 2022, with that of high-speed railway going up from 9,000 km to 42,000 km, still ranking first in the world.

 小结 Summary

词语 Words

根据课文内容，选择恰当的词语。Choose the appropriate words according to the text.

在启动刮板输送机时，司机首先要_____，确保其他人员离开转动部位，然后进行_____，判断运输机的运转_____。试运转时先按启动按钮，当刮板链运转_____后再停机。

A. 半周　　　　B. 试运转　　　　C. 方向　　　　D. 发出开机信号

语法 Grammar

朗读下面的句子。Read aloud the following sentences.

1. 确保其他人员离开转动部位。
2. 我们没有其他的检查方法。
3. 试运转正常了。
4. 煤电钻关停了。

课文理解 Text Comprehension

根据课文内容，判断对错。Tell True or False according to the content of the text.

司机启动刮板运输机时司机，不需要发开机信号。	A. 是	B. 不是
司机在开启刮板输送机前，要发出开机信号。	A. 是	B. 不是
当刮板运输机试运转时，要判断运输机的运转方向。	A. 是	B. 不是
试运转结束后，启动刮板运输机时应按两次启动按钮。	A. 是	B. 不是